Christian Higher Education in Northern India and Nepal as Revitalization Movements

Report on the Consultation on Christian Revitalization held in Dehra Dun, India, July 2014

Senior Editor: Robert A. Danielson

Assistant Editors: Roji T. George

R. Jeffrey Hiatt

Paul Tippey

Published by The Center for the Study of World Christian Revitalization Movements and First Fruits Press

Christian higher education in Northern India and Nepal as revitalization movements: report on the Consultation on Christian Revitalization held in Dehra Dun, India, July 2014.

Senior editor: Robert A. Danielson.
Assistant editors: Roji T. George, R. Jeffrey Hiatt, Paul Tippey.

First Fruits Press, ©2017

ISBN: 9781621715894 (print), 9781621715900 (digital), 9781621715917 (kindle)

Digital version at http://place.asburyseminary.edu/academicbooks/24/

First Fruits Press is a digital imprint of the Asbury Theological Seminary, B.L. Fisher Library. Its publications are available for noncommercial and educational uses, such as research, teaching and private study. First Fruits Press has licensed the digital version of this work under the Creative Commons Attribution Noncommercial 3.0 United States License. To view a copy of this license, visit http://creativecommons.org/licenses/by-nc/3.0/us/.

For all other uses, contact:

First Fruits Press
B.L. Fisher Library
Asbury Theological Seminary
204 N. Lexington Ave.
Wilmore, KY 40390
http://place.asburyseminary.edu/firstfruits

Consultation on Christian Revitalization (2014 : Dehra Dun, India)
 Christian higher education in Northern India and Nepal as revitalization movements: report on the Revitalization Conference held in Dehra Dun, India, July 2014 / senior editor, Robert A. Danielson; assistant editors, Roji T. George, R. Jeffrey Hiatt, Paul Tippey. -- Wilmore, Kentucky: Center for the Study of World Christian Revitalization Movements and First Fruits Press, ©2017.
  233 pages; cm.
  Foreword / Timothy C. Tennent – Acknowledgements / James C. Miller – The Northern Indian context / Roji T. George – The circle method / Bryan T. Froehle, Agbonkhiannmeghe E. Orobator – Case study one: Bharat Susamachar Samitit (BSS) and New Theological College (NTC) / Santhosh J. Sahayadoss – Case study Two: The Christian Evangelistic Assemblies (CEA) / Varghese Samuel – Case study three: Allahabad Bible Seminary / J. Sundera Raj, Thomas M.J. – Case study four: Nepal Ebenezer Bible College / Ram Kumar Budhathoki, Yeshwanth B.V., BP Khanal – Case study five: Native missionary movement / Erik Disch – Concluding remarks / James C. Miller.
  Includes bibliographical references.
  ISBN - 13: 9781621715894 (pbk.)
  1. Christian universities and colleges--India, North--Congresses. 2. Christian universities and colleges--Nepal--Congresses. 3. Education, Higher--Religious aspects--Christianity--Congresses. 4. Church growth--India, North--Congresses. 5. Church renewal--India, North--Congresses. I. Title. II. Danielson, Robert A. (Robert Alden), 1969- III. George, Roji T. IV. Hiatt, R. Jeffrey (Robert Jeffrey) V. Tippey, Paul Allen. VI. Center for the Study of World Christian Revitalization Movements.
LC432.I5 C66 2017   378/.071

Cover design by Jon Ramsay

First Fruits Press
The Academic Open Press of Asbury Theological Seminary
204 N. Lexington Ave., Wilmore, KY 40390
859-858-2236
first.fruits@asburyseminary.edu
asbury.to/firstfruits

Table of Contents

Foreward..1
Timothy C. Tennent

Contributors 5

Acknowledgements 9
James C. Miller

Chapter One: The Northern Indian Context 13
Roji T. George

Chapter Two: The Circle Method 31
Bryan T. Froehle and Agbonkhianmeghe E. Orobator, SJ

Chapter Three: Case Study One-Bharat Susamachar Samitit (BSS) and New Theological College (NTC)....................... 51
Santhosh J. Sahayadoss

Chapter Four: Case Study Two-The Christian Evangelistic Assemblies (CEA).. 83
Varghese Samuel

Chapter Five: Case Study Three-Allahabad Bible Seminary 117
J. Sundera Raj and Thomas M. J.

Chapter Six: Case Study Four-Nepal Ebenezer Bible College 141
Ram Kumar Budhathoki, Yeshwanth B.V., BP Khanal

Chapter Seven: Case Study Five-Native Missionary Movement 171
Erik Disch

Chapter Eight: Concluding Remarks 215
James C. Miller

Foreword

TIMOTHY C. TENNENT

Christianity on the sub-continent of India and Nepal is, by all accounts, a complicated and nuanced history. On the one hand, India is one of the few countries that can claim the presence of all seven major strands of Christian penetration. India has one of the strongest historical claims for an Apostolic introduction to Christianity with the arrival of St. Thomas to the Malabar coast in 52 A.D. India has also received multiple strands of Catholic witness, including Dominican, Jesuit and Franciscan. India also has a rich tradition of the Syrian Orthodox church, its depth demonstrated by the famous encounter of the "Croonan Cross." Later, India received the early Protestant witness of a long line of missionaries including Ziegenbalg and Plutschau, the famous Serampore Trio, Amy Carmichael, and many others, too numerous to count. After Independence, India experienced the full flowering of ecumenical Christianity, leading to the formation of the CNI and CSI church bodies, full members of the World Council of Churches. Finally, India has provided the soil for remarkable new Pentecostal and indigenous movements which have both re-shaped our understanding of Christianity in India.

Adding to this complexity, one must add that the majority of these seven strands were focused on South India, leaving North India and Nepal as, by comparison, untouched fields of Christian penetration. Thus, India is the home, simultaneously, of one of the oldest Christian movements on the planet (Mar Thoma) alongside numerous fresh, indigenous movements, like the CEA, which was one of the focal points of the Revitalization study. One also cannot ignore the dramatic differences: linguistic, cultural, caste, religious, and ethnic complexities in India, which have shaped the church and created significant barriers to the gospel's spread throughout India and Nepal.

One of the key findings of the Revitalization studies over the last seven years has been to dispel the notion of any such monolithic entity as "world Christianity" the way it is sometimes glibly used in missiological literature. What we, in fact, are finding through our global studies, is a rich tapestry of over 40,000 separate movements, all expressing both universality and particularity, in what is, today, known as world Christianity. Certainly, the traditional taxonomy of Catholic, Protestant and Eastern Orthodox as a simple rubric of understanding church history is no longer tenable as the growing Pentecostal and indigenous movements have so amply shown.

This volume brings the reader into intimate conversations with several indigenous movements in North India and Nepal. They provide a vital window into the complexity and beauty of Christianity in the sub-continent. Having dedicated much of my life to the expansion of the gospel in North India, I cannot fully express my joy in introducing some of these unknown movements to the larger church. I have had the privilege of working closely with these movements since their inception and the conversations that took place in North India, which these case studies illuminate, have shaped my own understanding of Christianity in profound ways. The story is fascinating and invites many new questions about how the church around the world is being re-shaped and re-presented in a vastly complex world.

Timothy C. Tennent, Ph.D.
President, Asbury Theological Seminary
Professor of World Christianity

Contributors

Rev. Ram Kumar Budhathoki, MA, M.Div, Principal, Nepal Ebenezer Bible College (NEBC), Kathmandu, Pastor, Srijana Church, Kathmandu, Nepal.

Abraham Cherian is a professor at Filadelfia Bible College, Udaipur City, Rajasthan.

Erik Disch is a mission co-worker with his wife and family in India, from Illinois in the United States.

Bryan T. Froehle is professor of practical theology at St. Thomas University, Miami Gardens, USA, where he directs the Ph.D. program in practical theology. Among his books are *Global Catholicism* (Maryknoll: Orbis, 2003).

Roji T. George is a professor of New Testament at SAIACS and a former assistant professor at Luther W. New Jr. Theological College.

Mr. BP Khanal, MA, MDiv, Faculty, NEBC.

Thomas M. J. is a faculty member of Allahbad Bible Seminary.

James C. Miller is Professor of Inductive Biblical Studies and New Testament at Asbury Theological Seminary in Orlando, Florida. He is the author of *The Obedience of Faith*, *The Eschatological People of God*, and *The Purpose of Romans*. Director, Center for the Study of World Christian Revitalization Movements

Agbonkhianmeghe E. Orobator, SJ, is provincial of the East African Province of the Society of Jesus, based in Nairobi, Kenya. Among his books is *Theology Brewed in an African Pot* (Maryknoll: Orbis, 2008).

Finny Philip is the principal at Filadelfia Bible College in Udaipur City, Rajasthan. He did his doctoral work at Durham University, where he obtained a Ph.D. in New Testament.

J. Sundera Raj is the principal of Allahabad Bible Seminary.

Santhosh J. Sahayadoss

Varghese Samuel is a member of the board and a pastor with the Christian Evangelical Assemblies.

Mr. Yeshwanth, B.V, B.E, B.D, Academic Dean, NEBC.

Acknowledgments

James C. Miller

The Case Studies at the heart of this volume were initially presented at the "Consultation on Christian Revitalization" held at New Theological College, Dehradun, India, from 29 July – 2 August, 2014. The Consultation was sponsored by the Center for the Study of World Christian Revitalization Movements (CSWCRM) at Asbury Theological Seminary in the United States and funded by a grant from the Henry Luce Foundation.

This Consultation was the second of four global research/Consultation events held in consecutive years in four non-Western regions of the globe. The first project studied East Africa, with a Consultation held in Nairobi, Kenya, in July 2013. The results of the Consultation have been published as Philomena Njeri Mwaura and J. Steven O'Malley, eds. *African Urban Christian Identity: Emerging Patterns* (Nairobi: Acton Publishers, 2015). Subsequent Consultations were convened in Manila, Philippines in July 2015 and San José, Costa Rica in January 2016. In other words, the research presented in this volume is one component of a unique, truly global research effort.

The project's design stems from thoroughgoing Trinitarian convictions. God the Father seeks to make himself known. The Father's clearest revelation has come through the incarnation of God's son. In other words, God's actions came with the smell of fish on its hands and Galilean dust on its feet. Today, God continues the work of Jesus Christ by the power of the Holy Spirit. But, as with Jesus Christ 2,000 years ago, that present day work takes place in specific cultural/historical contexts. In order to understand the work of God in our day, then, we must understand it in all its specificity.

The research attempts to listen carefully to stories of God's work today by use of two means. First, in each region, five case studies were conducted of churches, Christian movements, and/or Christian institutions. These studies were initiated up to 18 months prior to the Consultation. Secondly, the case studies were then prayerfully and carefully examined by interdisciplinary teams of scholars and practitioners over several days at the regional Consultation. The teams were interdisciplinary because a variety of perspectives – social sciences, history, theology, economics, etc. – were needed if the full context of each case was to be taken seriously. The teams examined the cases using the Pastoral Circle approach, an integrated method that allowed the team to reflect carefully over the course of their work together. In sum, we believe the case study research followed by interdisciplinary research Consultations offers an ideal tool for listening and discerning how God is at work in each particular context.

The leadership team for the entire project consisted of Dr. Jim Miller (Asbury Theological Seminary; Director of CSWCRM and Luce Grant Director), Dr. Bryan Froehle (St. Thomas University; Research Director), Dr. Paul Tippey (Asbury Theological Seminary), and Dr. Jeff Hiatt (Asbury Theological Seminary). Dr. Simon Samuel (New Theological College), Dr. Theresa Roco-Lua (Asia Graduate School of Theology; Asia Theological Association) and Dr. Wanjiru Gitau (Africa International University; Post-Doctoral Fellow CSWCRM) were part of the core leadership work at individual Consultations themselves.

The Consultation in Dehradun would have not been possible without the exceptional contributions of several people. Dr. Simon Samuel undertook the enormous task of organizing the Consultation on the ground at NTC. Dr. Bryan Froehle and Ryan Staples (videographer, Asbury Theological Seminary) made two advance trips to case study sites in order to mentor the case study writers and prepare video documentation for each case. The research and Consultation simply would not have happened without them.

NTC founder Dr. George Chavanikamannil, his wife, Leela, and the staff of NTC provided participants with exceptional hospitality. Our time together was truly a great joy in large part because of their servant spirit.

Robert Danielson, Paul Tippey, Jeff Hiatt, and Roji George took on the difficult task of editing a volume essays from contributors on multiple continents. Their work has made this result of the case study writers and Consultation participants available to a larger audience.

James C. Miller
Professor of Inductive Biblical Study and New Testament
Director, Center for the Study of World Christian Revitalization Movements
Asbury Theological Seminary
Orlando, FL, USA

Chapter One: The Northern Context

Roji T. George

India is a land of "Unity in Diversity." It would not be an exaggeration to say that after every few 100 kilometers one can witness differences either in language, ethnicity, religious practices, or culture in India. Yet, the history of Christianity in India, especially in South India, can be traced back to A.D. 52, when St. Thomas is believed to have come to the coast of Malabar with the gospel of Jesus Christ; the Christian presence in the northern part of India is known only after the arrival of the colonial nations, especially the British. Kerala witnessed several waves of Christian migrations through the centuries, but the northern belt of India remained unknown to Christ and his gospel until recent times. Christianity did not make significant inroads into places known today as Rajasthan and Madhya Pradesh. Its growth has been limited to pockets in various parts of North India in certain states.

To my dismay, I have yet to find a well-researched book on the history of Christianity in India that has a reasonable discussion on the growth of Christianity in Rajasthan and Madhya Pradesh, the two states from where two of our case studies are taken, in comparison to the space given to the Christian presence in South and Northeast India. Probably, this speaks at length about the relative absence or meager presence of Christianity in North India. Even today, the Christian presence in these states of North India is very small. The reasons could be manifold, including religious and social reasons that have hindered the growth of Christian mission. The case studies included in the present volume are important in this respect as they narrate their stories of overcoming challenges unique to their context in spreading the gospel of Christ.

In the remainder of this chapter, I shall seek to draw a broad picture of North India that can provide a broad background to assist someone unfamiliar with the region to understand, analyze, and appreciate each of the case studies discussed. I shall attempt to point out significant socio-cultural and religio-political factors of India that are vital for understanding the Christian mission from the perspective of a minority community.

Geo-Ethnic Diversity of North India: An Overview

To the north of India, Himalayan ranges run from north to east marking the boundary shared with Afghanistan, Nepal, China, and Tibet, while in the south, the land forms a peninsula covered by waters from the three sides. The western border of India is desert, while her eastern border is a mountainous region. India has a long history of civilization, often glorified, yielding much to the visible forms of diversity today. Even much of the present discourse on Indian identity, politics, and culture are carried-out based on the historical details. World religions like Hinduism, Buddhism, Jainism, Sikhism, Christianity, Islam, etc. have co-habited peacefully in India for centuries. As per the 2001 census, India, with more than a billion people living in it, has only a 2.3% Christian population.[1] In the political map of modern India, north India includes several states, namely, Rajasthan (in fact, the western border state), Madhya Pradesh (M.P.), Uttar Pradesh (U.P.), Uttarakhand (U.K. previously known as Uttaranchal), Delhi, Haryana, Punjab, Himachal Pradesh (H.P.), Jammu and Kashmir (J&K), Bihar, and Jharkhand. Of these, the four case studies compiled in the book come from the first five states. The Christian population in these states as per the 2001 census is below 1% (Rajasthan 0.12%; M.P. 0.28%; U.P. 0.12%; U.K. 0.31%; Delhi 0.94%).[2]

In these states of north India, the majority of the population follows Hinduism with important Hindu pilgrimage centers (like, Ujjain in M.P., Allahabad in U.P., Haridwar, Rishikesh, Bhadrinath, Kedarnath, etc. in U.K.) and ancient temples (including the ancient Brahmaji Temple in Ajmer, the Ghateshwar Temple in Kota, etc.) which make them vital to understand the growth and expansion of Christianity through the centuries. The three large states of India (Rajasthan, Madhya Pradesh, Uttar Pradesh), along with Delhi, have played a significant role in the political history of India from ancient times. Rajasthan, a land of "desert, rocks, lakes and jungles,"[3] has been a land of Rajputs (the ruling warrior class), Jats (Agrarian community), Gujars, and large tribes like Bhils, Meenas, and others. While the former have been, generally, dominant communities through the centuries, according to Gulahti, Bhil, "a carefree, romantic and chivalrous tribe," is "one of the oldest tribes of India" (also mentioned in the Hindu epics) who lived a secluded and exclusivist life style until the 19th century which "kept them primitive and backward." They follow Hinduism and the independent India government

---

[1] "Demographics of India," http://censusindia.gov.in/Census_And_You/religion.aspx (Accessed on 26/01/15).

[2] As per the India government census report 2001 Rajasthan has 72,660 out of 56,507,188 total population. Similarly, M.P. has 170,381/60,348,023; U.P. 212,578/166,197,921; U.K. 27,116/8,489,349; and Delhi 130,319/13,850,507 total population of Christians. See, "Population by Religious Communities" http://censusindia.gov.in/Census_Data_2001/Census_data_finder/C_Series/Population_by_religious_

[3] S.P. Gulahti, *Rajasthan*, in *Encyclopaedia of India*, ed. P.N. Chopra, vol. IV (New Delhi: Rima Publishing House, 1992), 3.

has paid special attention towards them for their social emancipation.[4] Similarly, adjacent to Rajasthan is Madhya Pradesh, the central region of India. Madhya Pradesh is famous for its rich ancient religious tradition and political heritage From the ancient time of *Mahajanpadas*, Madhya Pradesh has born witness to major political events even till modern times. Other than the *Varnas*, "a sizeable population of Madhya Pradesh is represented by several tribes and other backward people," who are scattered in various districts. The major tribes are Gonds, Jogis, Bhils, Mundias, Banjaras, and so on, of whom many claim to have their origin in ancient India.[5] Bhopal is the capital of Madhya Pradesh and one of the leading cities of the state along with Gwalior, Ujjain, and so on.

Another major state of north India is Uttar Pradesh out of which a smaller state called "Uttarakhand" was carved. Both of these states are important for they together hold several important Hindu religious sites where pilgrims flock everyday in the millions to take ritualistic baths or to perform various religious rites in the river *Ganga*. Major religious events like *Kumbhamela* are conducted in these cities. For Hinduism, these religious sites are immensely important in multiple ways. In Uttar Pradesh, there is also a huge presence of Muslims, predominantly, in the western part of the state. Social factors like caste and religious identity play a major role in the political arena of Uttar Pradesh. The earliest witness to the Christian presence in the state is traced back to 1578 when a Roman Catholic priest visited Agra. Thereafter, there were several other mission agencies that arrived in various parts of Uttar Pradesh.[6] On November 9, 2000, as a result of long-standing demand by the people of the region, a new state named "Uttarakhand" comprising of the hill districts in the north-west of the state was carved out in order to develop the region. Like U.P., Uttarakhand too contains several important religious sites like Haridwar, Rishikesh, Kedarnath, Badhrinath, Gangotri, and Yamunotri. Geographically, the state is divided into two major parts – the Garhwal and the Kumaun. While the majority of the population is Hindu, Muslims form the largest minority apart from Sikhs, Christians, and others. Rajputs form the largest group

---

4 Gulahti, *Rajasthan*, 54-56, cited from 55.
5 K.D. Bajpai, *Madhya Pradesh* in *Encyclopaedia of India*, ed. P.N. Chopra, vol. IV (New Delhi: Rima Piblishing House, 1992), 73.
6 B.N. Puri, *Uttar Pradesh*, in *Encyclopaedia of India*, ed. P.N. Chopra, vol. IV (New Delhi: Rima Publishing House, 1992), 54-55.

of people, while approximately 20% of the total population comes from the lower castes of the Hindu *Varna* system.[7]

With such a diversity of people inhabiting a large geographical area of India, we need to understand the resultant socio-cultural state of the society today. How have these diverse groups of people lived together for centuries? Have they cross-fertilized each other culturally to make the present cultural terrain of north India such a complex field to carry out Christian mission? What are the socio-cultural challenges confronting Christian missionaries today?

A Broad Sketch of Socio-Cultural Evolution of North India

The Indian sub-continent has a long history of civilization, dating back to the third millennium B.C.E. in the Indus Valley or Harappan Civilization (2300-1750 B.C.E.), which spread concentrating on the coastal regions from southern Punjab and Sind to the Narmada delta.[8] Although in the past a large group of historians contended for an Aryan invasion theory for the decline of the Harappan civilization, in the current discussion most reject this theory in favour of a large migration of people called "the Aryans" from central Asia with a distinct language called "Sanskrit," at a later period. The Vedic culture and religion which forms the core of Hinduism spread throughout north India with their later eastward movement.[9] Manu Bhagavan contends that "[t]he Harappan civilization began to regionalize around 1900 B.C.E., an event that eventually resulted in the dissipation of the urban-centered culture of the region."[10] Several settlements and later kingdoms (the famous sixteen *Mahajanpadas*) and Empires (like Maurya, Gupta, etc.) grew along the Indus and Ganga valleys like the Gandhara Grave culture in Northern Punjab, the Banas culture in Rajasthan, the Copper Hoard Culture in southern Bihar and West Bengal, etc. They prove that over the period of time, several cultures mushroomed in an interconnected way without a single

---

7 Raj B. Mathur, "Uttarakhand," http://www.britannica.com/EBchecked/topic/736432/Uttarakhand (accessed on 29/12/2014).
8 Romila Thapar, "Society in Ancient India: The Formative Period," in *Readings in Early Indian History* (New Delhi: Oxford University Press, 2013), 82.
9 Thapar, "Society in Ancient India," 82-92; Manu Bhagavan, "The Historical Context," in *Understanding Contemporary India*, eds. Sumit Ganguly and Neil DeVotta (New Delhi: Viva Books Private Limited, 2003), 19.
10 Bhagavan, "The Historical Context," 19.

dominant culture "which slowly spread throughout northern India bringing the various diverse cultures into its fold."[11]

Several waves of foreign invasions, including the Islamic invasion of the Medieval times and the British invasion after the arrival of the East India Company, along with the migrations of people from the Northwestern Asiatic regions created a mixture of people, cultures, and religions. At the earliest stage of the Islamic invasion, Mahmud Ghaznavid invaded India only to amass wealth. Hence, he looted various Hindu temples, such as Somnath, for its wealth and also to assert victory over the local deity. According to Bhagavan, "they plundered temples to expand their sphere of influence, they often plundered temples, not only to fund their military campaigns ... but also to strike at the symbols of leadership of their local opponents."[12] However, later during the reign of Iltutmish (a Slave dynasty in Delhi), in order to escape from the Mongol ruler Genghis Khan, a large number of scholars, poets, and artists migrated from Iran to the subcontinent. "This influx of talent into India brought with it a period of dynamic cultural change."[13] It created a mutual cultural influence between Hinduism and Islam, which during the later times, is evident in the Hindu bhakti and Sufi traditions. Even Akbar, a famous Mughal ruler, influenced by such cultural hybridization attempted to create "his own personal spiritual path, the Din-e-Ilahi (divine faith)."[14]

However, by advancing from the Aryans through the Vedic period to the present, Hinduism has evolved as a religion of the majority in the Indian subcontinent. The important contribution of the Vedic system to the Indian social system is the *Varna* System (Caste System) which divides the entire society into four major parts – *Brahman, Kshatriya, Vaishya,* and *Shudra* – with hundreds of subcastes (*jatis*). Under this system each caste has a specific economic function prescribed, so that, the *Brahmans* are assigned priestly duties, the *Kshatriyas* are the warriors and the rulers, the *Vaishyas* form the trade and commerce group (the business people), and the *Shudras*, considered to be the lowest among all the *Varnas*, are peasants and small artisans who perform the manual labour. However, apart from these castes was a large group of the untouchables/the Dalits who are accorded less than human dignity and are landless labourers. These subcastes are "endogamous and culturally distinct status groups" which are mostly visible in "the realm of religion and

---

11 Thapar, "Society in Ancient India," 83.
12 Bhagavan, The Historical Context," 25.
13 Bhagavan, The Historical Context," 27.
14 Bhagavan, The Historical Context," 31.

religious ritual" where each of the *varnas* is assigned distinctive ritualistic functions and each one is separate from the other by strict purity-pollution rules along with other rules guiding socio-religious reciprocity between the four major castes and subcastes.[15] For centuries, this social arrangement guided the society which even today influences daily life within the society, including those of Muslim, Christian, Sikh, or any other religion. Vibha Pinglé rightly states that the Hindu caste system has influenced the minority religious groups to a great extent that even their social religious interactions have been guided by similar social patterns.[16]

In the post-independent India, although the strong grip of the caste system has been weakened by various governmental interventions and legal provisions protecting the weaker section of people, but the caste system makes its strong presence felt by regular reports of honour killing, resistance by the upper castes over the dalits' entry into various temples, etc. However, the reality is that the democratic political system has empowered the dalits to subvert the upper caste dominant electoral politics by forming various political parties such as *Bahujan Samaj Party* (BSP). The *Shudras*, dalits, and tribals together formed the two-third's of the population in 2000, in contrast to the upper caste who formed only 18 percent of the total population. Reckoning their numerical strength and the impossibility of having a viable political system at the cost of the lower castes' interests, all the political parties have sought to adopt an affirmative action policy safeguarding the interests of the lower castes. These changes along with the new phenomenon of regrouping among the lower castes for political domination have hugely impacted the socio-economic condition of the marginalized people. Today, with governmental measures like job reservations, reservation for the underprivileged castes and tribals in educational institutions, laws against any form of discrimination of the low caste people based on their caste identity, etc. the low caste people have begun to compete with the upper caste people in various realms of public life.[17]

Although such a socio-cultural hybridization is a historical reality in India amidst communities preserving their unique cultural differences and social divisions as essential to their communal existance, in recent times the national political discourse has taken a different path of discussion. In recent decades, the

---
15 Vibha Pinglé, "Caste," in *Understanding Contemporary India*, eds. Sumit Ganguly and Neil DeVotta, 233.
16 Pinglé, "Caste," 235-237.
17 Pinglé, "Caste," 237-246.

rise of right-wing political parties with strong Hindutva ideologies have dictated the political discourse by defining national identity in narrow/exclusivistic terms. It has seemingly possed huge challenges/threats to the minority communities like Christians and Muslims in India. I firmly believe that any discussion on the Christian missionary endeavor as "Christian Revitalization Mission" must be discussed in the context of this recent political phenomenon.

A Religio-Political Context of Christian Mission in Post-Independent India

Down through the centuries, north India has continued to witness the socio-cultural, religious and political changes and development which played an important role even in the modern religio-political discourse. In recent years, the polyethnic, multi-religious history of India has become the ground of major debates and dissentions in terms of national policy. It has, seemingly, supplied ample ammunition to the right-wing cultural: religious, and political ideologues to assert a narrow definition of national identity. It has constantly led to divisive politics and the polarization of people based on religious identity and communal violence. Even now, as I am writing these introductory remarks, the national media in the nation is debating on issues such as: (i) communally charged hate speeches and the use of foul language (such as calling minority community members *Haramzade* meaning "illegitimate children" of India as opposed to Hindus who are *Ramzade* meaning "Children of Ram") by the elected members of the parliament from the ruling political party and people with a certain ideological allegiance against minority communities, (ii) vandalization and desecration of churches, (iii) forced conversion and/or conversion through allurement allegedly done by Christian and Muslim missionaries while the accusers of the majority community are themselves accused of resorting to the same conversion tactics under the banner of *Ghar Vapasi* (Home Coming/Returning) in places like Agra (Uttar Pradesh), Allapuzha (Kerala), Bastar (Chattisgarh), etc., (iv) creating an atmosphere of fear among minority religious communities (especially, of Semitic origin), (v) racist attacks upon North-East Indian students in various cities, (vi) dictates against women regulating their freedom to dress and move freely in society by certain fringe groups with political patronage, etc. Interestingly, these ideas are discussed or debated more vigorously in these days than the development plank ("*Sab ka Saath, Sab Ka Vikas*") with which the recently elected Central Government led by Prime Minister Narender Modi came into power.

Since independence, India has professed to be a secular nation of which the underlining philosophical principle is defined as *Sarva dharma, Sama bhava* ("Equal Respect for All Religions"). Nevertheless, the nation has also witnessed the constant rise of right-wing Hindu religious and political groups, which advocate a narrow ideology of Hindutva that prioritized Hindu identity as the national identity. Hindutva, as a reactionary movement, had its beginning in the pre-independent India under the British colonial regime, which attained an organisational structure and strong ideological underpinning in the twentieth century. Within Hinduism, it has had a reformist agenda and intends to forge unity by downplaying the Hindu Caste System, rationalizing Hindu beliefs, and developing a communal consciousness/identity to counter foreign religions, like Christianity or Islam. Hindu nationalism began to witness a turn towards militancy through the formation of various organizations championing the Hindu cause, like Hindu Mahasabha, Rashtriya Swayamsevak Sangh (RSS), Vishwa Hindu Parishad (VHP), Bajrang Dal, Shiv Sena, and the political arm of Hindutva, the Bharatiya Janata Party (BJP). Hindu nationalism owes its origin to the insensitive Christian missionary works from pre-independent India, the British colonial recognition of the Hindu community, and Orientalism.[18] In the present scenario, the greatest challenge the Christians of modern India face is the resurgence of Hindu cultural-political nationalism.

The Hindu identity, which has evolved over many years, holds the key to their understanding of 'Indian-ness' as 'Hindu-ness.' The three vital variables of the Hindu identity claimed by the proponents of Hindutva are territory/geographical boundary, religion, and caste or language.[19] Within this framework, the Hindu identity is constructed both in inclusive and exclusive terms. It means that Hindu, a geographical term, is used "not only for those who were living across the Indus river,

---

18 M.T. Cherian, *Hindutva Agenda and Minority Rights: A Christian Response* (Bangalore: Centre for Contemporary Christianity, 2007), 156-153; Robert Eric Frykenberg, "Hindutva and the Aftermath of Ayodhya: Dangers of Political Religion and Religious Nationalism," in *Nationalism and Hindutva: A Christian Response*, ed. Mark T.B. Laing (Delhi: ISPCK/Pune: CMS/UBS, 2005), 5-12.
19 T.K. Oommen, "Religious Nationalism and Democratic Polity in India: Impossibility of Reconciliation," in *Nationalism and Hindutva: A Christian Response*, ed. Mark T.B. Laing, 36-37.

but also for those who professed a religion other than Islam or Christianity."[20] This definition of Hindu was substantiated by reinterpreting Indian history as Hindu history, eulogising Hindu heroes, such as, the mythic king named Vikramaditya, Shivaji, and Maha Rana Pratap, over Mughal emperors, and eternalising the Hindu/Hinduism as *anadi* (without beginning) or *Sanatan dharma* (eternal religion).[21] Even the most agressive communal violence between Hindus and Muslims in post-independent Indian history, the fall of Babri mosque in Ayodhya in December 1992, has been the direct consequence of the religous-political claims made based on past historical details. The mosque, built by a Mughal emperor named Babur in the sixteenth-century, was demolished claiming it to be built on the same site as Lord Rama's birthplace where the mythic king Vikramaditya (some confuse him with Chandra Gupta II) is said to have built a temple dedicated to Rama at the direction of the god Prayag. The spread of violence has been a result of deep-rooted animosity between the two communities and the longlasting dispute over the religious site.[22]

Rashtriya Swayamsevak Sangh "emphasizes that Hindu culture is the national culture. Hindu society is national society, Hindu art is national art. Hindu literature is national literature and Hindu history is national history. People belonging to various religions (excluding Christianity and Islam) in this country are all Hindu by culture and are nationals of this *Hindu Rashtra*."[23] Foundational to the Hindu claims is that the Hindus are the original inhabitants of the land. It forges unity and co-opts the native cultures or religions (the *Mlechhas* and *Adivasis*)[24] into Hinduism, a mosaic of varied sects, cults, castes, peoples, and cultures. However, the Hindutva ideology is antagonistic towards the religions of non-Indian origin, and caricatures these by misrepresentation as foreign and the agents of foreign

---

20 PralayKanungo, *RSS's Tryst with Politics: From Hedgewar to Sudarshan* (Delhi: Manohar, 2003), 92.
21 Kanungo, *RSS's Tryst with Politics*, 90-127.
22 Bhagavan, "The Historical Context," 21, 29-30.
23 Kanungo, *RSS's Tryst with Politics*, 126-127, (Parenthesis added). The term, *Rashtra*, in Hindi, means 'Nation.'
24 The proponents of Hindutva have used the term 'Hindu' all inclusively but it is a known fact that the indigeneous people, the *adivasis* and others have maintained a non-Hindu identity. See John D'Mello, "Letting the Converted Speak...: Towards an Emic Approach to Conversion," *JPJRS* 3/1 (2000): 6-11. For a discussion on Hinduisation of Adivasis and Dalits see Arjun Patel, "Hinduisation of Adivasis: A Case Study from South Gujarat," in *Dalits in Modern India: Vision and Values*, ed. S.M. Michael (New Delhi: Vistaar Publications, 1999), 186-212; Ebe Sunder Raj, *The Confusion Called Conversion*, rev.ed. (New Delhi: TRACI Publications, 1998), 86-92, 115-118.

powers with colonial intent. The primary reason for such a fear is that the Christian missionary activity would threaten the Hindu majority status through conversion. The proponents of Hindutva are outspoken about the Hindu identity in essentialist, dominant, and imperialistic terms which threatens to annihilate every other cultural identity. Hence, according to Frykenberg, Hindutva

> is certainly very modern. Proselytising and political in character, chauvinistic and imperialistic in demands, and defensively aggressive and militant in attitude, it claims to 'represent' *all* the 'noble' and 'pure' peoples of India; and it calls for the subordination and subjugation of all defiling or non-pure peoples of India to Ram Rajiya. In short, its protagonists have given new name and new meaning to the term 'Hindu'. In the name of '*Hindutv*', or 'Hindu-ness', advocates for this kind of 'Hinduism' insists that they not only speak, in statistical terms, for a mythic '*Hindu majority*' but also that this majority, *which only they alone can represent*, by virtue of cosmic fiat (*vishwadharm*), must have sole control and total dominion over all that lies within the territorial bounds of the subcontinent of 'India' or 'Aryavartha'.[25]

As a result, Hindutva objectifies *Swaraj* (self-rule) as the final goal. The '*Swa*' meaning 'we' refers to the Hindus who are perceived to be the original inhabitants of India, the enlightened (Aryans), in whose hands is the governance of the *rashtra* envisaged. It is the centre, the Hindu 'Self,' that constructs the margins, the 'Other,' who are termed as "uncivilized and barbaric."[26] It underlines the conflictual relationship between Hindutva proponents and Christians. The proponents of Hindutva have argued that the "Christian missionaries are only trying to further their political ambition in the name of God and religion, and that their activities are not merely irreligious but also anti-national."[27] Christians have been accused of destroying the Hindu *sanskriti* (culture) by imposing Western culture, dress, worship pattern, and so on, upon the indigenous peoples. Christians are accused of maintaining transnational loyalties without a sense of pride in belonging to the *janmabhoomi* (the land of birth), i.e., India/Bharat.[28] The zealous evangelization resulting in conversion done by the Christian missionaries, both in the pre- and

---
25 Frykenberg, "Hindutva and the Aftermath of Ayodhya," 14.
26 Kanungo, *RSS's Tryst with Politics*, 94.
27 Kanungo, *RSS's Tryst with Politics*, 114.
28 Kanungo, *RSS's Tryst with Politics*, 114.

post-independent era, among the Dalits and Adivasis has been viewed with suspicion. The foreign funds received by the Church in India are alleged to be used for alluring the depressed groups of people aiming to convert them. Often, the theological terms employed to elucidate the execution of the Great Commission of the Lord Jesus Christ is quoted out of context, fuelled by political meanings.[29] These malicious misinterpretations of Christians in India and the missionary task undertaken by the Church have provoked widespread persecution of Christians across the nation, similar to Gujarat, Orissa, and Madhya Pradesh.

Moreover, in the past there has been a constant demand for the Uniform Civil Code and an Anti-Conversion Bill by the members of the majority community in order to curb the missionary activities of the minority communities as well as to superimpose a majority cultural identity upon the minority to project a single national identity. Often the Hindu hardliners have viewed the minority communities as disrupting communities who by not yielding to conform or assimilate with the majority disrupt national aspiration. But the fear of the minority of "being overwhelmed by the majority community is expressed even in opposition to the making of homogeneous civil laws. These are treated as threats to a specific culture and practice."[30] Perhaps, the latest addition to such fears is the central government's decision to celebrate the 25th of December as "Good Governance Day" coinciding with the birthday of the former Prime Minister, a true statesman, and the leader of the BJP, Mr. Atal Behari Vajpayee. Although the government rejects every claim of ulterior hidden motives behind the move, the fear and suspicion of the Christian minority is of the new government's fresh move to impose the majory view by force upon the minority community. Undoubtedly, there is a huge deficit of trust with the BJP led government among the Christians.

Finally, it is in this complex context that we need to understand the Christian Revitalization Movements spearheaded by various Christian organizations in north India. The struggles they face in reaching the unreached with the gospel of the Lord Jesus Christ are born of socio-cultural, religio-political, and other forms of practical hindrances. While continuance of India as a democratic, secular, and

---

29 For example, Lobo mentions the misinterpretation of Pope John Paul's speech in 1999 arguing that "the pope is going to overturn India in the third millennium." Lancy Lobo, *Globalisation, Hindu Nationalism and Christians in India* (Jaipur and New Delhi: Rawat Publication, 2002), 28.
30 Romila Thapar, "Imagined Religious Communities," in *Cultural Pasts: Essays in Early Indian History* (New Delhi: Oxford University Press, 2000), 986.

religiously tolerant sovereign nation is essential for the Christian mission, the case studies selected in this compilation prove that the proclamation of the gospel in the present cannot be oblivious to the social realities such as social inequality, economic deprivation, the religious divide, gender discrimination, etc. India requires a gospel that is culturally coloured, socially relevant, economically empowering, and religiously sensitive; the need of the hour is a complete re-incarnation of Christian missionary practices in the Indian context. The case studies prove their revitalization mission and demand due attention in these areas without which the Christian propagation of the gospel will not yield the desired result.

Works Cited

Bajpai, K.D.
    1992   "Madhya Pradesh." in *Encyclopaedia of India*, ed. P.N. Chopra, vol. IV, New Delhi, India: Rima Publishing House, 1992.

Bhagavan, Manu
    2003   "The Historical Context," in *Understanding Contemporary India*, eds. Sumit Ganguly and Neil DeVotta. New Delhi, India: Viva Books Private Limited.

Census of India (Ministry of Home Affairs)
    2001   "Demographics of India," http://censusindia.gov.in/Census_And_You/religion.aspx (Accessed on 26/01/15).

    2001   "Population by Religious Communities" http://censusindia.gov.in/Census_Data_2001/Census_data_finder/C_Series /Population_by_religious_communities.htm (Accessed on 26/01/15).

Cherian, M.T.
    2007   *Hindutva Agenda and Minority Rights: A Christian Response*, Bangalore, India: Centre for Contemporary Christianity.

D'Mello, John
    2006   "Letting the Converted Speak...: Towards an Emic Approach to Conversion," *JPJRS* 3/1 (2000): 6-11.

Frykenberg, Robert Eric
    2005   "Hindutva and the Aftermath of Ayodhya: Dangers of Political Religion and Religious Nationalism," in *Nationalism and Hinutva: A Christian Response*, ed. Mark T.B. Laing, Delhi, India: ISPCK/Pune: CMS/UB.

Gulahti, S.P.
    1992   "Rajasthan," in *Encyclopaedia of India*, ed. P.N. Chopra, vol. IV, New Delhi, India: Rima Publishing House.

Kanungo, Pralay
    2003   *RSS's Tryst with Politics: From Hedgewar to Sudarshan*, Delhi, India: Manohar.

Lobo, Lancy
    2002   *Globalisation, Hindu Nationalism and Christians in India*. Japiur and New Delhi, India: Rawat Publication.

Mathur, Raj B.
    2012   "Uttarakhand," http://www.britannica.com/EBchecked/topic/736432/ Uttarakhand (accessed on 29/12/2014).

Oommen, T.K.
    2005   "Religious Nationalism and Democratic Polity in India: Impossibility of Reconciliation," in *Nationalism and Hindutva: A Christian Response*, ed. Mark T.B. Laing, Delhi, India: ISPCK/ Pune: CMS/UBS.

Patel, Arjun
    1999   "Hinduisation of Adivasis: A Case Study from South Gujarat," in *Dalits in Modern India: Vision and Values*, ed. S.M. Michael, New Delhi, India: Vistaar Publications.

Pinglé, Vibha
    2003   "Caste," in *Understanding Contemporary India*, eds. Sumit Ganguly and Neil DeVotta, New Delhi, India: Viva Books Private Limited.

Puri, B.N.
    1992   "Uttar Pradesh," in *Encyclopaedia of India*, ed. P.N. Chopra, vol. IV, New Delhi, India: Rima Publishing House.

Raj, Ebe Sunder
    1998   *The Confusion Called Conversion*, rev.ed. New Delhi, India: TRACI Publications.

Thapar, Romila
    2000   "Imagined Religious Communities," in *Cultural Pasts: Essays in Early Indian History*. New Delhi, India: Oxford University Press.

    2013   "Society in Ancient India: The Formative Period," in *Readings in Early Indian History*. New Delhi, India: Oxford University Press.

Chapter Two: The Circle Method

BRYAN T. FROEHLE AND AGBONKHIANMEGHE E. OROBATOR, SJ[31]

---

31 This work is based in part on papers and workshops presented separately by Orobator and Froehle in Nairobi on July 18-19, 2013. Many thanks to Paul Tippey, Jeff Hiatt, and James Miller for insights and critical feedback that have greatly strengthened this work.

Summary

After an initial series of consultations on World Christianity that included gatherings during Edinburgh 2010 and in Toronto, Asbury Theological Seminary's Center for the Study of World Christian Revitalization Movements initiated a second series of case-based consultations in East Africa, South Asia, East Asia, and Latin America. The consultations are rooted in an incarnational approach and build on the Circle Method, one full of promise for the study of World Christianity.

Contextuality

What is God doing today around the world, and what is God asking of Christians and the world Christian movement today? How are Christians responding to God's call, and how are societies changing? What is new in the world Christian movement, and what are important trajectories for the future?

Such general questions are often given an equally general response. One may move deductively, from general principles to specific instances, of course. But there are good reasons to be suspicious of such an approach, since it often treats accidents of history and assumptions that are often hidden as normative, missing that all generalizing is done from within some specific context. Scholars then become 'merchants of abstractions' rather than advancing understanding of concrete experience or following as disciples of an actual Person. Alternatively, one may proceed inductively, building up understanding from within a particular context. This approach to understanding is the one taken in considering the questions named above.

These concerns are at the heart of the design and conduct of the consultations on the reality of world Christianity designed by Asbury Theological Seminary's Center for the Study of World Christian Revitalization Movements (CSWCRM). What follows describes the methodology of the consultations and discusses the Circle Method, which is at the heart of the consultations themselves.

Methodological Reflections

Approaches to World Christian Studies

The growth and challenges faced by Christianity around the world today may be studied from many different disciplines, all of which have something important to say. Demographic studies that look at the levels of affiliation and participation across time and place offer new consciousness about the global reality of Christianity. General historical narratives within particular countries or regions (Frykenberg 2010; Hartch 2014) as well as confessional or denominational contexts have offered new in-depth descriptions of the trajectory of Christian life. The discipline of religious studies has brought its narrative, descriptive focus along with its sensitivity to the comparative study of meaning systems behind diverse traditions. Political and social studies of various kinds have explained political implications and social transformations tied to various contemporary Christian expressions around the world. Finally, theological approaches have provided insights critical to understand emerging Christian self-understanding in contemporary contexts around the world.

Such approaches as these are all helpful in their own right, but limited. They often tend toward a focus that is more general than specific, more an outsider than an insider perspective, and about a single disciplinary approach rather than an intradisciplinary one.

The Consultation Approach

For these reasons, the CSWCRM developed its consultation approach. Designed to examine world Christian trajectories -- that is, areas of renewal or revitalization, growth or innovation within world Christianity today -- each consultation is aimed within a specific cultural geography, with a preferential nod toward urban contexts, given global population realities. By itself, this already brings a stronger sense of context. Each consultation engages very specific cases of "revitalization" movements. Thus, the "case" is the unit of analysis for advancing understanding of world Christianity. In other words, the approach is resolutely inductive from beginning to end.

Each case is ideally a local level expression with features of renewal, revitalization, innovation, or growth. They are chosen to complement the others featured during the consultation as well as those considered in previous and planned consultations. Placed in conversation with each other, the cases are open to comparison and in-depth consideration in their own right. Above all, the goal for each consultation is not a predetermined set of comparisons or assumptions but a conversation that advances theological and social understanding in an integrated manner. A critical part of this conversation is between the cases themselves, even while acknowledging that these cases themselves may be influencing the conversation. All levels, including this level, are therefore subject to a hermeneutic of suspicion (Gadamer 1984, Baltodano Arroliga 2013).

Outsider perspectives offer the possibility of a claim of "neutrality" but typically sacrifice insider insight. This is all the more problematical in areas so richly imbued with meaning, such as religion, that oftentimes only insiders can fully appreciate them. The solution cannot be a simple preference for a pretense of neutrality, however. All research by human beings with human beings involves some particular personal perspective in any case. Third party objective observation is simply not something humans can do. On the other hand, a purely insider approach also misses critical questions or understandings precisely because insiders naturally take their own reality for granted. So -- instead of the typical model of the single outside scholar-researcher, a combined insider-outsider approach that engages multiple voices, including insiders, offers opportunities for deeper insight and new levels of collaborative learning.

The limitation to a single discipline needlessly impoverishes – even imprisons -- understanding, all the more when theological or religious questions are at the heart of the inquiry. As already noted, without contextual understanding, theology is inevitably segregated into a space of speculation and abstraction. However, mere contextual understanding from experience alone brings an impoverished understanding of theology that cannot substantially advance the theological conversation. Further, engaging theology as a single discipline leads to the simple uncritical adoption of insights from other fields, denying the discipline a theoretical or methodological capacity of its own. After all, as an interpretive science, theology does not stand on its own but walks with and from dialogic partners in other disciplines (Osmer 2008).

THE CONSULTATION MODEL: A METHODOLOGICAL RESPONSE

The consultations are designed to advance learning from patterns of revitalization and transformation in the global south and east by understanding the context of specific cases of revitalization movements, whether within congregations or wider networks of churches, or within specific forms of parachurch organizations, or other forms. They collect data, quantitative and qualitative, on emerging initiatives or developments, seeking to help resource the emerging needs of theological education by providing narratives and paradigms that help understand contemporary directions in world Christianity.

Such an approach offers an opportunity to build symbiotic relationships between academic settings globally so as to develop reciprocal learning ventures. In these ways, the consultations help Asbury Theological Seminary's Center for the Study of World Christian Movements fulfill its mission to "contribute to the vitality of Christian mission and local congregations by synthesizing learnings from past and present revitalization movements worldwide."

INSTITUTIONAL BACKGROUND

Every method has a specific origin, one that must be understood if the method is to be understood. The method in this case flowed from a project to explore the revitalization of the church in urban cultural contexts in Africa, Asia, and Latin America. Specifically, the project consists of four consultations – Nairobi, Kenya; Dehradun, India; Manila, the Philippines; and San Jose, Costa Rica. The consultation model is therefore oriented toward encountering the Christian message at the intersection of religious and social change in the particularities of these contexts. Based at a leading Wesleyan institution for theological education, the Center naturally has another, ancillary goal focused on the relationship between renewal movements and theological education. This relationship is critical. Insofar as theological education is designed to produce church leaders, those leaders must be able to engage and lead movements of revitalization. In addition, given the Wesleyan movement's situation at the point between diverse ecclesial contexts and expressions historically and its rootedness in questions of praxis from its beginnings in John Wesley, Asbury Theological Seminary is a particularly appropriate point of origin and inspiration for this project.

Consultation Design

Each consultation includes approximately 40 participants representing a diversity of backgrounds and intersecting disciples as academics, theological educators, church leaders, researchers, and renewal movement leaders. These participants are grouped into five teams, or "circles," each of which is assigned one of the five cases over the days of the consultation. These groupings are designed to consist of some eight members in all, two of whom are the writers and leaders who prepared the initial report, with the rest from as wide a diversity as possible of backgrounds and experiences in scholarly disciplines and ecclesial leadership, reflecting a wide range of Christian traditions. The learnings of the consultation are then shared broadly within the context of a public event immediately after the consultation. Speakers at the public event are those who served as overall synthesizers within the consultation, above and beyond the role of the individual teams. These are typically scholars in world Christianity or leaders within Asbury, the Center, or the project as a whole. Additional dissemination after the public event takes place in the form of publication of a volume on the cases and local context, as well as an overall text on the project and videographic work on individual cases and talks from the consultation or public event.

Approximately a year before the consultation, each case selected for study is given over to two key collaborators who will be eventually presenting at the consultation and serving within one of the circles as the voice of that particular circle's case. These two collaborators are both writers and leaders – that is, the leaders may themselves be writers or the writers may be an engaged scholar who works with a leader to draft the initial study received and read by participants about two months before the consultation. The team members represent a variety of scholarly disciplines and/or ecclesial leadership experience. They come from different Christian confessions and theological understandings, but all bring a common commitment to understand the case at hand in the most fulsome way possible so as to advance together both social and theological insight.

The consultation has five such teams and thus a total of approximately 40 participants as well as overall leaders and coordinators who do not serve on any particular team. All participants, not simply the team members, receive the written case study materials in advance. All participants receive and review brief audiovisual presentations of the cases prior to the start of the team meetings at the consultation. This is to provide more in-depth understanding of their particular case but also a comparative framework across all the cases.

Throughout the consultation, the comparative dimension continues in a dynamic way. At various points between the team sessions, all participants gather together as a single group to discuss and hear reflections from the other cases together with comments and critique from designated discussants on particular issues that likely cut across the cases. At the end, the process is heightened with collective consideration of emerging themes, even while recognizing that those themes themselves are limited to the specific backgrounds, contexts, and approaches of those present and the specific cases selected for the consultation.

The final, crowning public event of the consultation engages many times more persons than the participants themselves. At a larger public event, which can include special subgroupings depending on the context where the consultation takes place, insights generated during the consultation are shared with ecclesial and other leaders. Consultation participants and designated spokespersons from each team offer their new clarity about each of the five cases and theologically-imbued interpretations and correlates of those cases, together with provisional conclusions and insights generated through the consultation process.

The main work of the consultations, and therefore the great bulk of the meeting time, is dedicated to each specific case. Each circle works on moving toward greater insight in interpreting the case from both social and theological perspectives. This is facilitated by the initial paper, which is revised and expanded after the consultation to reflect the learnings, including responses to important questions raised by the team and above all the theological insights that emerged. This process depends on very involved circles meeting over five different sessions, the first four of which are designed to correspond to the four main movements of the circle method. The fifth session is devoted to evaluation and summary for purposes of the consultation itself.

The Circle Method

Movements within the Method

The Circle Method can be traced to the hermeneutic circle (Segundo 1972) and pastoral circle (Holland and Henriot 1981; Wijsen, Henriot, and Holland 2005; Wijsen 2005), among many other sources. This format or ones like it, have been widely used now for many decades, and the form goes back to basic ways of human understanding that can be traced down through the ages. Many variations of this approach exist, particularly within practical theology, and it is known by many names (Osmer 2008; Browning 1991; Whitehead and Whitehead 1995).[32] It is often called the "pastoral cycle" (Green 1994) or "spiral" (Wijsen 2005) to refer to a dynamic, transformative quality. Its origins and applications can be traced across history and in many different contexts.[33]

The Circle Method offers a particularly appropriate structure to the consultation, given that it seeks case-based, collective, and intradisciplinary forms of insight. It offers a dynamic way of proceeding for theological reflection, beginning and ending in action. As used in the consultation, it takes the form of a structured conversation that allows for mutual learning and shared insight from insiders and outsiders, scholars and practitioners.[34] In many ways, the method is not particularly different from approaches to knowledge-building implicitly found in the Scriptures or throughout Christian history. The movements of the method are found in ordinary practices of Christian discernment critical for leadership and scholarship, prayer and contemplation. It is found in some form within contemplative spiritualities, particularly those oriented toward discernment, including discernment in the context of Christian discipleship and vocation. Each context and people group that has engaged in this method adds something unique to its understanding, however, and the African context is no different.

---

[32] Within Africa, the Circle of Concerned Women Theologians (http://www.thecirclecawt.org/) regularly uses this method, following the influence of Mercy Oduyoye, as do other pastorally inflected theologians and ministers throughout the continent.

[33] This method is often used to seek out the relationship between faith and justice. In a Catholic context, roots go back to Catholic Action and the "see-judge-act" approach popularized by Joseph Cardijn.

[34] In this way it builds on associative learning approaches, one of the most basic ways of human knowing.

Calling the method a "circle" is particularly appealing in an African context due to the traditional ways of decision-making found in African villages. All would gather in a circle and offer words of insight from their perspective. This palaver, or circle sharing, is very much at the heart of this practical theological method. If, as has been said, theology is a "team sport,"[35] the same is particularly true for this method of producing insight (Lonergan 1992). Each aspect of the method can also be plotted as a movement along a circle, one that effectively has neither beginning nor end, and which includes within it all aspects of the method. Ultimately, the movements are not meant as a recipe but rather as dynamic moves toward ever greater insight and more sure action. They are not so much a structure or machine for producing knowledge – which is then inevitably reified – nor are they so many specific phases or steps. Rather, the "movements" simply represent elements or aspects on which focus should be given for a time to ensure that collective discernment is as complete as possible.

The Circle Method is named, then, not for a "circle" of steps to be completed or cycle to be followed nearly as much as the circle of people who engage it as in, for example, the consultation. Rather than imagining these movements as ones to be diagramed – though they can be – they are best understood as fundamentally to help ensure that basic building blocks of insight are not missed or slighted in some way. Each such movement is therefore more heuristic than distinctive, and there can be no insistence that the movements necessarily must always proceed in the same stepwise order. Ordinary human ways of learning and proceeding simply vary too much by situation, human choice, and their own internal and external logics to insist on any one such flow. Though the order of movements given here implies a certain logic, others exist: this is not the only one. Further, the reality is that each "move" inevitably contains within it in some way elements of the other movements – they cannot be separated one from another without hopelessly reducing the entire process to a lifeless abstraction. The Circle Method is about *phronesis* – practical wisdom – and as such makes its path by walk rather than a preset formula.

First Movement: Identifying and Inserting

The initial focus is on the "what" of the case. What is happening? It seeks to tell the story at first glance, while at the same time identifying the actors involved

---

[35] This follows Terrence Tilley's formulation. See http://www.ctsa-online.org/pdf_doc_files/Tilley%20Citation.pdf.

and showing how they, including any 'outside' researchers, are inserted into the case and its context. This movement, then, has a strong incarnational component, recognizing that God is present already in the situation. One both 'inserts' oneself in a reality, and one finds that one is already inserted in it! To separate oneself from reality, after all, is merely heuristic: one is always part of reality and not separate from it. Action occurs within other actions, tied to a cascading, interrelated host of actions. Part of the work in this movement is about identifying one's position and biases so as to be suspicious of them. Spiritual discernment, for example, calls to the comfortable to see how God sees – from the perspective of all God's people, including most particularly the poor and marginalized on the underside of history (Gutierrez 2004). Questions characteristic of this movement ask where and how one pitches one's tent, which must always be a response to where God has pitched the divine tent (Sobrino 2008).

Questions that may be helpful in this movement include the following: What is the setting of this case, including geographic, social, cultural, and other factors? What stories do people tell about themselves and the case of which they are a part? What organization(s) and organizational stories are part of the case, including origins, developments, and structures? What people and personal profiles are part of the case, including leaders, members, insiders, and outsiders? What understanding of God, God's action, and Christian renewal is part of this case?

Second Movement: Assessing and Analyzing

The focus in this movement is toward understanding why and how the case has developed as it did. It involves a particular blend of discipleship and discernment, requiring explanatory lenses that bring together personal and social frames.

Sometimes young children can innocently ask "Why?" – a question they follow up with another "Why?" and still another. One way of thinking of this movement is to think of it as a dynamic encounter with this "Why?" question asked many times over, as an inquisitive child might.[36] This requires bringing a particular questioning of one's own actions, or that of one's group. Such actions and understanding must be held in a certain suspicion if one is to respond to the "Why?" question as fulsomely as possible.

---

36 This is the same approach used in Six Sigma. See http://www.isixsigma.com/tools-templates/cause-effect/determine-root-cause-5-whys/.

Sometimes one can show these relationships in diagrams and tables, in carefully constructed sentences and paragraphs. However, these cannot be the final word – such dissection can become a lifeless, bloodless exercise. Tables and diagrams do not suffer and weep, nor can they laugh and smile. The focus of this movement, as with the Circle Method as a whole, has to be incarnational, never separated from the only place where God can be found – in God's creation, among God's people. Reality is revelation is relationship. This movement is about seeing relationship more clearly, not breaking it into pieces.

Questions that might be helpful in this movement include the following: What is really going on within this case overall, from a "bird's eye" view? What specific difficulties and opportunities does the organization and people face, and how have they acted? How might observers analyze or theorize about the situation and actions undertaken? Where can divine action most readily be seen in this situation?

Third Movement: Correlating and Confronting

This movement emphasizes meanings and interpretations, ones that both inform and form. Consistent with the method, it looks at the interplay of understanding so as to further advance understanding. It links the development of understanding within the particular case to theological concepts, Biblical stories, and broad Christian themes. Insofar as God's revelation of Godself is encountered in creation itself (King 2005), this calls for a broad, sacramental view open to the surplus of meaning in the encounter with God in everyday life. There is always more to be understood. This movement is ultimately about the art of play in linking understandings.

Using analogy (Tracy 1998), one of the most basic human forms of knowing, a different order of theological reflection arises – one already emerging in the other movements but which is here distinctively configured (McBrien 1994: 732). In some ways, what might appear to be a move to abstraction is a move to greater specificity: the correlations or affinities seen here lead to confrontations as one is caught up short, both personally and in the context of a particular case. A clear confirmation of this movement is in feelings of awe and surprise, a sense of being animated by the Holy Spirit to see things differently and more completely (Elie 2004: 256-258).

Some questions that might be asked in this movement include:

What theological or Biblical concepts, stories, or meanings can be related to this case? What person, church, or other experiences can be related to this case?

How does this situation challenge or expand specific understandings of Biblical/theological truth or experience?

What deeper understandings of theological/Biblical truths seem to be emerging from exploring this case?

Fourth Movement: Empowering and Extending

The central question here is about next steps, the kind consistent with conversion or *metanoia*. There is a sense of being empowered and compelled toward action. In this movement, the critical question is quite simply 'What to do?' In a pastoral context, the focus would be on pastoral planning and strategic action. In any case, the normative dimensions of this are explored in all the other movements, but perhaps most intensively in the correlating-confronting movement. If this is more generally oriented toward theological and social understanding, then the action component might be more about actions that extend further understanding. There is an element that must always be both personally and socially transformative. Revitalization is communal, always more than mere structural adjustments – it is about conversation that reshapes action as ongoing praxis. Thus this is more than simply a pragmatic or strategic move.

Questions that might be useful in this movement could include the following: How does this new insight deepen energy for Christian renewal? What are the next steps for leaders and scholars, both in their own action and in the collective actions of which they are part? What could limit leaders and scholars in these next steps? What new kinds of cases or new questions is God prompting for future consideration?

Fifth Movement: Evaluating and Summarizing

This flows from the needs of the consultation itself, since it contemplates a collective consideration of multiple cases. The key question here is "What should we say?" Its goal is to put forth and refine the major, critical conclusions of the work of the team so that they might be briefly presented by the team members to all participants, and ultimately, after seasoning within the wider discussions at the conclusion of the consultation, at the ensuing public event. There is another goal in this as well, and that relates to the resulting paper on the case that will emerge from this consultation. This will be a revised and expanded version of the original paper first presented to the team and consultation participants by the writer and the writer's collaborators. As a result, the product that flows from this needs to be as smart, tightly worded, and strongly presented as possible. Ideally, it will blend story with context and theological-biblical themes and understandings.

Questions that might be useful in this movement could include the following: What are the main take-aways from each of the four case sessions? How can this case be best summarized before the larger group? What directions for practical action and scholarship exploration does this case suggest for Christian renewal? How have these consultation case sessions been helpful, and how could they be improved? How has the circle method been helpful and how could its use be improved?

Conclusion

The methodological aspects underlying the consultations on World Christianity offer an opportunity to intentionally link case studies with theological work. In this way, the study of World Christianity is not merely descriptive and analytical but interpretive, ultimately directed toward understanding where the Christian tradition is being stretched and pulled. Those in theological education may find this approach not only an expression of practical theological method but a source of insight for the next generation of pastoral leaders in a wide diversity of contexts.

APPENDIX: THE CASE REPORT FORMAT

This appendix is provided to show the share of the paper that project collaborators submit on their case prior to the consultation. This paper is meant to serve the circle method design used in the consultation. After the consultation, it will be revised to incorporate learnings that emerged from the use of the circle method during the consultation.

The paper should be about 20 pages, double spaced, with additional pages for a bibliography and notes. Each paper should focus on a single case, though there could be references to other cases' discussion of the context. The paper must have a strong and clear discussion of difficulties or lessons learned rather than focusing only on successes. Headings (centered and in bold) and subheadings (to the left and in bold) should be used, but the headings and subheading should contain no numbering. *The Chicago Manual of Style* (sixteenth edition) should be used.

First Section: Definition

About two pages of an approximately 20 page narrative, this beginning section names and describes the case selected for study as a revitalization movement (perhaps a congregation, or "movement," or something else); this single case is the unit of analysis for the paper. It should identify the mission and vision of this case as understood today by its leaders or others, as appropriate, and show why the case merits particular attention.

Second Section: Context

About four of approximately 20 pages, this part of the work names and analyzes critical elements of the general social setting as well as the religious and church setting. Other similar or contrasting cases may be mentioned in passing here, but the focus of the remaining paper must be on the single case selected for study.

Third Section: Development

The single largest portion of the work and will be about 9 pages in length. It must have a strong analytical focus on how the organizational and leadership structure developed as they did. It should also provide strong focus on history and personal stories should be limited and emphasize difficulties and lessons learned from challenges and changes.

Fourth Section: Learnings

This portion is about 4 pages in all. It names and analyzes major areas or learning for Christian revitalization suggested by the study. It also proposed provisional linkages of these learnings to theological understandings, Biblical concepts and stories.

Fifth Section: Future

This final section is about two pages and presents especially significant lessons learned by the writer from the case. It also explores possible changes or adjustments in thinking or strategy for this case or Christian revitalization suggested by this case.

Works Cited

Baltodano Arroliga, Sara.
    2014   "La Circulariodad Hermeneutics en Teologia Practice Rompe El Espejismo del Paradigma Positivista." Pages 397-432 in *Pensar, Crear, Actuar* – V y P 33, 2 (2013) Y 34,1 (2014). San Jose, Costa Rica: Universidad Bíblica Latinoamericana.

Browning, Don
    1996   *A Fundamental Practical Theology: Descriptive and Strategic Proposals.* Minneapolis, MN: Fortress Press.

Elie, Paul
    2004   *The Life You Save May Be Your Own: An American Pilgrimage.* New York: Farrar, Straus, and Giroux.

Frykenberg, Robert
    2010   *Christianity in India: From Beginnings to the Present.* Oxford: Oxford University Press.

Gadamer, Hans-Georg
    1984   "The Hermeneutics of Suspicion," *Man and World* 17: 313-323.

Green, Laurie
    1994   *Let's Do Theology: A Pastoral Cycle Resource Book.* New York, NY: Continuum.

Gutierrez, OP, Gustavo
    2004   *The Power of the Poor in History.* Maryknoll, NY: Orbis Press.

Hartch, Todd
    2014   *The Rebirth of Latin American Christianity.* Oxford: Oxford University Press.

Holland, Joe and Peter Henriot, SJ.
    1983   *Social Analysis: Linking Faith and Justice.* Revised and enlarged edition. Maryknoll, NY: Orbis Press.

John Courtney Murray Award
    2012   Citation in honor of Terrence W. Tiley. http://www.ctsa-online.org/pdf_doc_files/Tilley%20Citation.pdf (Accessed 6/6/2017).

King, SJ, Thomas M.
    2005   *Teilhard's Mass: Approaches to "The Mass on the World."* Mahwah: Paulist Press.

Lonergan, SJ, Bernard
    1992   *Collected Works of Bernard Lonergan, Volume 3. Insight: A Study of Human Understanding.* Toronto, Canada: University of Toronto Press.

McBrien, Richard
    1994   *Catholicism.* New York, NY: HarperOne.

Osmer, Richard
    2008   *Practical Theology: An Introduction.* Grand Rapids, MI: Eerdmans.

Segundo, SJ, Juan Luis
    1976   *The Liberation of Theology.* Translated by John Drury. Maryknoll, NY: Orbis Press.

Six Sigma
    n.d.   "Determine the Root Cause: Five Whys." http://www.isixsigma.com/tools-templates/cause-effect/determine-root-cause-5-whys/ (Accessed 6/6/2017).

Sobrino, SJ, Jon
    2007   *No Salvation Outside the Poor: Prophetic-Utopian Essays.* Maryknoll, NY: Orbis Press.

Tracy, David
    1998   *The Analogical Imagination: Christian Theology and the Culture of Pluralism.* New York, NY: Crossroad.

Whitehead, James and Evelyn Eaton Whitehead
    1995   *Method in Ministry: Theological Reflection and Christian Ministry.* Revised Edition. Lanham, MD:. Sheed and Ward.

Wijsen, Frans, Peter Henriot, SJ, Rodrigo Mejia, SJ, eds.
    2005   *The Pastoral Circle Revisited: A Critical Quest for Truth and Transformation.* Maryknoll, NY: Orbis Press.

Wijsen, Frans

    2005   "The Practical-Theological Spiral: Bridging Theology in the West and the Rest of the World." Pages 108-216 in Wijsen, Frans, Peter Henriot, SJ, Rodrigo Mejia, SJ, editors. *The Pastoral Circle Revisited: A Critical Quest for Truth and Transformation.* Maryknoll, NY: Orbis Press.

50

Case Study One: Bharat Susamachar Samitit (BSS) and New Theological College (NTC)

Santhosh J. Sahayadoss

Abstract: Bharat Susamachar Samiti (BSS) and NTC (New Theological College) are indeed revitalization movements. The founders took a deliberate and conscious effort to establish a movement that is unique and different from other movements and subsequently attempted to create a counter culture that can impart significant new values to society, the church, and to theological education in India. This movement had a gradual but strong impact on the members of this group who have become partners with the founders in fulfilling the mission and vision of these institutions.

DEFINITION

The entire BSS, NTC, and CEA (Christian Evangelistic Assemblies) story has its beginning in God's call, commission, and confirmation to Uncle George and Aunty Leela Chavanikamannil. Their simple desire was that many should hear the gospel so that the unreached *Jathis* of India would have a chance to hear the gospel of Christ in this current age. Uncle George has narrated the story of how he and Aunty with George C. Kuruvilla (Babu Bhaiya) took on the adventure of finding the land, the people, and the resources to start this project from a humble beginning. At the beginning of this ministry, Uncle George was unable to comprehend if this would be a "small" risk taken for God's kingdom or whether this initiative guided by God would bless the lives of many North Indian people through building the kingdom of God and become a significant educational and ecclesiastical institution in India. He had the confidence from his early days when he resigned from World Vision, because of surprising experiences that emerged from this desire to start and establish a ministry in North India. He received his initial vision at the age of 19 in Kerala, but the fact that this burden, which the Lord gave him to start a ministry in North India, would grow by leaps and bounds within a brief period of time and become a revitalizing movement was the result of his being obedient to this call.

Some of the surprising twists and turns that took place at the beginning of this ministry, and which led Uncle George and his wife to be confident that this new movement was from the Lord, included a number of key events. First, was Uncle George's initial boldness to resign his job at World Vision and the way God prepared George C. Kuruvilla (Babu Bhaiya) to join him in the early stages of establishing this ministry that led them to feel this was from God. In addition, the whisper of the words *"Jehovah Jireh"* in the ears of Uncle George by a pastor's wife prompted by the Holy Spirit during the Annual Conference of the CEA, in Roseburg, Oregon in October 1985, gave more confidence in God's provision. God's guidance through Pastor Ray Eicher to settle the ministry in Dehradun, as well as the cooperation Uncle George received from the Christian leaders in Dehradun in welcoming him and affirming his call, was an important stepping-stone for the ministry. The generosity of World Vision, USA to publish an article about this ministry for the sake of fund raising, and Pastor Steve Riggle's suggestion to make a model of the proposed campus, which was made without seeing the land, were important steps of faith. Finally, the financial resources to buy five acres of land, along with the owner's willingness to sell at a price prayed for by Aunty Leela, as well as God's help in bringing human resources to support Uncle George, helped the vision come to life.

Bharat Susamachar Samiti (BSS) was registered as a society in 1987, particularly to train young men and women to spread the good news of Jesus Christ to every *Jathis*. One of the first projects of BSS was to establish New Theological College. Through this institution, BSS has trained many Christians to become evangelists and preachers of the gospel. The founder believed that the best way to reach India with the gospel is by training national Christians. There are specific reasons why the founder believed that training national Christians is important. First of all, foreign missionaries are no longer permitted in India. Second, the founder asserted that national Christians are far more effective in communicating the love of Jesus to their brothers and sisters in India. Third, it must be pointed out that supporting a local missionary is much easier financially than supporting Western missionaries. In the place of supporting one Western missionary, twenty to forty national Christians can be supported. Fourth, since Hindu religious fundamentalism is rapidly increasing, opposition to preaching the gospel is also on the increase. This situation makes it nearly impossible for Westerners to preach the gospel in India. Finally, the founder believed that well-trained national Christians could contribute much to the growth of the Indian church than others. With these aims in mind, BSS established one of its first training centers in India, New Theological College. Dr. Ted Engstrom, President Emeritus of World Vision, dedicated NTC on April 15, 1989. In the beginning, there were only 22 students who joined for training at NTC. However, at present, NTC has become a fully accredited evangelical theological seminary in North India with nearly 260 students. NTC along with the help of its satellite training centers has produced nearly 2000 qualified missionaries, who are willing to serve in India and build the Indian Christian church. NTC is affiliated to the Senate of Serampore and also fully accredited by Asia Theological Association, and offers Bachelor and Master degrees in Theology. In addition, some special courses like a Certificate Course in Theology, a Diploma in Worship and Music in the School of Music and Worship, and linguistics training in the Institute of Languages and Linguistics are offered for those who want to be trained here. Courses are offered both in Hindi and English.

Drawing inspiration from the commandments, "Love thy neighbor as thyself," and "Let the little children come to me and do not hinder them," young men and women after their graduation from NTC ventured into rural and semi-rural areas to reach out and touch the lives of young people by giving them a "Christ-centered" quality education. In 1990, Pastor Regi John, one of our CEA pastors, was burdened to start a school in Pathri for the sake of the discriminated, neglected, and abandoned Dalit people of North Indian society. This resulted in constructing a school in Pathri that was named *Good News Academy*. Later on this same group of men and women guided by the founding fathers and mothers established *Jeevan Jyothi Bal Vikas* (Life and Light Child Development). This is an organization that helps extremely poor Dalit children to learn to read and write, and in the process teaches Bible stories to them. This beginning in *Pathri* marked the growth of interest in the BSS leadership to start many more schools and projects for children in this area. Through these institutions and organizations the gospel of Jesus Christ was shared and many have come to the saving knowledge of our Lord and Savior Jesus Christ.

CONTEXT

At the beginning of this ministry, BSS was established to provide ministerial training and theological education to equip young people to motivate them to reach the unreached. This was and is the original vision, and NTC is directly connected to this original vision. The Mission Statement of NTC reads:

> We exist to serve the church of our Lord Jesus Christ in the Indian sub-continent. Our mission is to train spiritually alive, professionally competent, and socially relevant Christ-like servant-leaders for the church at all levels. The focus of our training is equally on "heart" (character), "hand" (skill), and "head" (knowledge). We pledge to

constantly guard against the temptation to over-emphasize the importance of "head" and sacrifice "heart" or "hand."

Similarly, the Vision Statement of NTC states:

> We plan to train large numbers of Christ-like servant-leaders primarily for the church in the Indian sub-continent as the harvest here is plenty and laborers are few. For this we will follow the example of our Lord Jesus Christ: first of all by living the gospel by depending on the grace of our Lord Jesus and with the help of the Holy Spirit. We will be examples to the ones we train in word and deed. We will work hard, doing everything as unto the Lord (Ephesians 6:7). We will whole-heartedly obey the Golden Rule that our Lord taught us: "Therefore, however, you want people to treat you, so treat them, for this is the Law and the Prophets" (Matthew 7:12).

The focus of NTC is to serve the whole church and society in the power of the Holy Spirit. There is an intense interest in preserving a spirit of inter-denominationalism, evangelicalism and charismata. There is a healthy mixture of evangelicalism and ecumenism. Likewise, BSS as the parent organization of NTC believes social transformation can only be achieved through communities of believers who are committed to transforming our society and nation so that all can truly worship God. BSS desires to make this dream come true. The best we can do for India is to preach the gospel of the one who loves all, irrespective of whether they are Dalits or Brahmins, Poor or Rich, Educated or Uneducated. God loves all alike and expects us to love all in return. Intimacy with God (the vertical dimension) must be evidenced by intimacy with fellow human beings (the horizontal dimension). Only then does the cross become complete.

DEVELOPMENT

District of Haridwar- Bharat Susamachar Samiti (Reported by M.I. Kuriakose)

Bharat Susamachar Samiti is a movement acting as an "agency" of change in society with a vision to empower and educate the downtrodden and marginalized. It has started two schools, two projects, and a children's home in this district in Pathri and Bhagwanpur. In 1990, BSS started the first school in a rented facility in Pathri with hand full of children and called it "Good News Academy" under the leadership of Rev. Reji John, who was primarily involved in planting churches in this area. In the year 2007, BSS started Jeevan Jyoti Bal-Vikas (Light and Life Child Development) project for holistic development of the children of these marginalized communities.

BSS started a second school in another area, Bhagwanpur, in the year 2004 under the leadership of Mr. Dinesh Kumar. This school is called "Krisht Jyoti Academy" (Bhagwanpur) and started in a small way, at first as a project of BSS with 60 pupils in the first year. Along with the school they have also started a hostel for the children of new believers. At first, four children were admitted, and the teachers took care of them. In 2010, BSS started a child development project Jeevan Jyoti Bal-Vikas in this area for the overall development of the needy children of this community.

These schools have state recognition till eighth grade and authorities are pursuing the CBSE recognition for twelfth grade. At present, we are involved in a fivefold ministry in this district. First, the schools in these needy and backward areas cater to the educational needs of the children. Second, the Jeevan Jyoti Bal-Vikas project is an empowering agency that is facilitating holistic development of the children of this community through complimentary interventions, free education, and income generation programs through self-help groups. Third, the children's home in Bhagwanpur is a place where the younger generation is groomed in Christian leadership. Fourth, the David C. Cook program started in Bhagwanpur is a method of imparting solid spiritual teaching to these children. Fifth, the church-planting ministry in these villages is also making its progress, which is the missional goal of BSS.

The progress of this movement has been steady and has impacted this society socially, economically, and spiritually. The mission movement was started with a clear vision to bring renewal and change to this society, where all sorts of discrimination prevailed. These communities were neglected by the Government agencies and pushed to live on the fringes of society, avoided by socio-economic and religious systems. There was no social control over these communities, and no one was there to monitor their life pattern. So, immorality, alcoholism, illiteracy, and other evils crept into the social fabric of this community, which caused a deterioration of the social values enshrined in the Indian ethos. For example, the *sapera* (snake charmers) were nomads who subsisted on begging and stealing. They were marginalized people who were living in darkness. But BSS mission movement penetrated into the everyday life situations of these innocent, illiterate communities and brought awareness about the way they were exploited and other evils that they encountered. After imparting this awareness, they began to settle down and started building a community for themselves. Now they know the value of education and their children are studying in our English medium school.

Mr. Balakar, formerly a snake charmer, availed the help offered by our "income generating" program initiated by one of our projects and setup a small provision store for his community. Earlier he was a nomad and subsisted on begging and stealing. Now his family has settled down in this place and his child is receiving a good education in the school and progressing in life. Our mission movement is also involved in Dalit empowerment by helping this community to acquire free loans in order to start agricultural work. Ravinder, a small farmer, received help from this facility and cultivated sugar cane. This helped him to come out of the clutches of the moneylenders who exploited him and to resist the forces that marginalized him.

Moreover, the ministries of BSS helped these communities to understand the need of empowering women. To achieve this goal, BSS schools encouraged the education of girl children of marginalized families. They were given free English medium education through the school with the help of the project. Over the years, BSS workers brought awareness concerning child protection policies and introduced special care for children. They took steps to stop child labor and child marriage. They even helped people who wanted to become financially stable to have their own fixed deposits and opened saving accounts for their children in the nearby bank. "Income generation" programs were made available for women of the community so that they may become self-reliant. "Jyoti Self Help group" is one such group established by BSS that helps women. Eleven women in that Dalit community in Bhagwanpur are given training in toy making and now they have their own bank accounts. Now they are able to save some money and support their families.

All these social and economic programs in these communities enable the BSS movement to also do spiritual ministry among them. Fifteen churches were planted in the nearby villages and the ministry is self-supporting. The church among the snake charmers is one among the first to be established. This community has built a thatched shed under which they worship, and 60 people gather every Sunday for worship in this House of Prayer (*DuaKaGhar*). New believers are systematically taught Biblical truths through church worship and monthly meetings. Constant teaching and encouragement is needed to sustain the faith in the given situation due to social situations and religious opposition. For the staff members, retreats and other meetings are organized to keep their enthusiasm level high, and they are provided guidance and counseling in their difficult ministry situations.

Bhagwanpur ministry (Reported by M.I. Kuriakose)

Krisht Jyoti Academy, Bhagwanpur, the second school created by BSS, was recognized by the government in 2006. At present, the school has classes up to the eighth grade, with 32 children (all children of new believers) in the hostel and three staff members rendering their services in the hostel. The limitation of space constrains us from giving more admissions to the hostel even though there are many needy children in the village churches. Our goal is to mentor these children so that they may become leaders of the local churches in the days to come. Along with the school ministry, the members of this movement planted churches in the villages. Now we have planted ten churches in this area, and the main church gathers on the school premises every Sunday. In the year 2010, BSS started a child development project in this area for the overall development of the needy children of this community. At present, 185 children are benefiting from this project, with plans to admit 70 more children in the coming days.

When the school was started in a rented building, four children of new believers opened the way to relate with the community. The staff literally visited the villages and encouraged the parents to admit their wards in the school. They also were able to gain the trust of the Muslim community in this area who sent their girl children to the school. In fact, the Muslims in this area were initially not open to the education of girl children, but there has been a rapid growth of this ministry within the past ten years.

Simultaneously, the church-planting ministry was started giving importance to house visits and praying for the sick. A few of the relatives of new believers opened their homes for prayer in the nearby villages, and the members of the staff visited them and started Sunday worship in their houses. A few of the neighbors and their relatives who came and attended these meetings received Christ. In 2013, we were able to baptize 22 people. In the area of church-planting work, this movement has grown very fast due to much hard work. In January 2014, a youth camp was conducted for the church members in this area.

Garhwal Region/ Rudraprayag District- Bharat Susamachar Samiti (Reported by Abraham C. Thomas)

Bharat Susamachar Samiti has been functioning as an agent of change and renewal through its educational and philanthropic projects in the Garhwal region of the state of Uttarakhand for the last two decades. Garhwal is situated in the Northwestern region and is the administrative division of the Northern Indian state of Uttarakhand, which is the home of the Garhwali people. This report deals with the ministry of BSS in two hill districts of Garhwal region, namely Tehri Garhwal and Rudraprayag.

BSS runs a school and a training center in the Tehri Garhwal district and another school in the Rudraprayag district. Mount Carmel Christian Academy, Narendra Nagar (Tehri Garhwal) was started in 1997, with the vision to impart education to the people of Garhwal. Dr. Chacko, the founder of this school, used to carry relief materials to the earthquake affected people in Uttarkashi and the pass through Narendra Nagar. Knowing of his interest in education, the people of Narendra Nagar approached him to start a school, and so, a co-educational, English medium school was started in a rented building with almost fifty students in its first year. In 2005, Bharat Susamachar Samiti purchased a piece of land and developed a beautiful campus for the school with all the facilities needed for a high school.

Mount Carmel Training Center, Narendra Nagar was started in 2001, under the leadership of Rev. Samuel P. Rajan, a graduate of New Theological College, to give grassroots level ministerial training to young men from the Garhwal region. At first, the training program was six months, but later it was extended to one year. Every year ten young men enrolled for the training and were equipped to preach the gospel and plant churches in the unreached areas of the Garhwal region. This training center was instrumental in preparing young local men for church planting work. Today, there are almost fifteen churches/house churches and hundreds of believers in the Garhwal hills as a result of the ministry of these young men.

Krisht Jyoti Academy in Rudraprayag was started in 2006. This school was started in response to a specific vision that God gave to Rev. Ashish Khandelwal, one of the NTC graduates, during a prayer visit to this place in 2003. The school was started with just 3 students, but today there are 450 students enrolled. It is now one of the best schools in this region.

Both schools were established in areas where there were no good English medium schools offering quality education. These places only had government Hindi medium schools that were not up to the mark. For many people in this area, receiving good quality English medium education was a distant dream, as they were economically poor and socially backward. Through BSS schools, this dream became true, because BSS schools offered good quality education for everyone irrespective of gender, caste and creed at an affordable cost or even free for some. The school authorities had to deliberately and consistently address the caste issues in society and affirm the dignity of every human being, and thus empower the Dalit community by providing the best education possible.

Another issue the schools had to address was the education of girl children. In many of these places, people had no interest in educating their girl children. The BSS schools could really address this issue through consistently working with the parents. Today there are almost an equal number of boys and girls in these schools. Moreover, BSS has always believed that imparting quality education, which brings radical transformation to every aspect of the child, is the only permanent and lasting solution that helps to constructively respond to the various unjust issues that we face today as a nation. These schools are committed to imparting a quality education aimed at the all-round development of the students.

New Theological College (NTC) (Reported by Sooraj Pal, New Theological College)

New Theological College has made a phenomenal impact on the lives of young people who came here for theological studies. In the beginning, NTC offered a five months course on "Discipleship," and anointed men of God trained the young men who registered for this course. The outcome of this endeavor was that nineteen of the young people who joined the course were baptized. Then NTC went on to offer a one-year course. The probability of starting a theological school was not in the hearts and minds of the founding fathers and mothers in the early stages.

The Student's Handbook: Guide of Conduct outlines some of the core aspects of NTC that direct students:

The college (NTC) is willing to give scholarships for needy students. However, there is a minimum grade requirement for students on scholarship. There is also a minimum attendance requirement. If a student misses more than 20% of the classes, he/she will be asked to discontinue his/her studies and may be permitted to rejoin in the same semester next year. Plagiarism or copying in assignments or examinations is a violation and serious disciplinary action will be taken. If any student fails in more than 50% of the subjects then he/she has to redo that year of studies. Attendance is taken in the library during library hours. Students who are irregular will be called before the disciplinary committee. Students who receive a scholarship must be willing to do scholarship work. Otherwise, they can pay the amount at the end and release themselves from the ministry commitment period. Silence should be maintained during study hours in the evening.

Students are not allowed to go to the city during the working week. They are also not allowed to visit cinema halls. Gambling and occult practices are strictly forbidden. Students are not allowed to stay outside the campus without permission. There must be modesty in dressing. Any unhealthy relationship with outsiders will be reproved. There shall be no private talk between a male and a female student. Any kind of immoral relationship will lead to termination of the students involved. Students shall avoid all physical contact with another student. There shall be no hugging between male and female students. Besides these rules and regulations, the students are instructed to participate in the early 5:30AM morning chapel for students, 8:00AM chapel for all, evening chapel for students, Abba father prayer time twice a week, and one full day fasting and prayer every month. All these programs must be attended apart from the lecture hours. Those who miss any of these appointments without proper permission will have to appear before the disciplinary committee. The use of cell phone is strictly forbidden.

In many theological seminaries and colleges in India and abroad, importance is given to academic performance, just like in secular colleges. This can be a dangerous pitfall for anyone who is in the process of being trained for church ministry. There is a greater chance of students graduating with lots of head knowledge and little heart knowledge. So, Uncle George has been instrumental in inculcating Christian piety in the lives of students through Abba Father Prayer meetings for students and staff, and faculty prayer meetings for staff and faculty periodically, twice a week for students, and twice a month for staff and faculty. NTC observes a fasting and prayer day once every month to nurture the spiritual life of all. The students are trained to participate in early morning devotions and evening devotions. Everyday, there is also a common worship for students, staff and faculty. Through these rigorous spiritual disciplines, Uncle George and the leaders believe that quality leaders will emerge who will take the Indian church in the right direction.

Uncle George also believes in working together with others and cooperating with one another in the mission field. He is against identifying any one denomination as the "true" Church. Rather he would see all genuine Christians as part of the body of Christ. Consequently, mission becomes the passion of all Christians and the most important task of the church. Partnership with others becomes very significant in accomplishing this task of the church. Uncle George would take the risk of partnering with others for the sake of fulfilling the mission, even if there are some doctrinal differences with these partners. However, submission to the authority of the Holy Scripture and following the apostolic faith are non-negotiable. In spite of these basic conditions, Uncle George has many friends and partners in ministry from the Roman Catholic and Orthodox traditions, as well as different Protestant denominations, such as Methodists, Lutherans, the CSI, and the CNI Church traditions, as well as some Baptists and Pentecostals.

Uncle George focuses on two important aspects of Christian ministry. One is to plant churches among *Jathis* where the gospel is not yet proclaimed. Second, he does not wish to build on another's foundation. He is also aware of the opposition that can come and is coming from others because of the social and political changes taking place in India, primarily the growth of Hindu religious fundamentalism that is against the spread of the gospel of Jesus Christ. Under his leadership, neither BSS nor NTC nor CEA has buckled down under this increasing pressure. He and his partners, along with his faithful co-workers, believe that India is a secular nation wherein everyone has the right and freedom to profess, propagate, and practice one's own religion. This is a basic freedom and a human right. Even though the threat of persecution is always there, particularly from those who are enemies of the Gospel.

Understanding the Indian context well, Uncle George knows that the need in India is diverse. The need in the cities is entirely different from the need in rural areas. On the other hand, training theologically sound pastors to meet these needs has become a costly affair. From the inception of NTC, the focus was primarily on training evangelists to meet the demand in rural areas. In the beginning, only one-year certificate courses were offered. In quick succession, a Bachelor in Theology and Divinity, and a Masters in Divinity and Theology were added to the programs that the college offered. Even though higher levels of theological education have been recent developments, the one-year certificate course, training evangelists to meet the needs of rural areas has not been abandoned. Uncle George was highly disappointed when the Bachelor in Theology taught in Hindi had to be scrapped because of a low number of applicants. He always tells the highly qualified faculty and well educated students from the cities that they should not look down upon students who come from poor, rural backgrounds, and that they should embrace, honor, and serve such students from humble backgrounds.

NTC also aims to make its contribution to the theological fraternity at the national and international levels, as evangelicals, have made steady progress in their theological articulation of concepts and ideas that are unique and special to them. NTC publications: *Remapping Mission Discourse* and *DTJ* (Doon Theological Journal) are evidence of the ability of NTC faculty to reflect on important theological issues of today. In fact, NTC has, from the beginning, encouraged the students, staff, and faculty to research and write articles on themes that are unique every year. Under the leadership and guidance of Rev. Dr. Simon Samuel, the Principal of NTC, the *Doon Theological Journal* has made steady progress in publishing excellent articles twice a year. Rev. Shivraj Mahendra, a convert, who studied at NTC and later has become a faculty member, has been engaged in translating a number of theological text books from English into Hindi, so that the Hindi speaking community can benefit. In this regard, it is worth making note that all official programs of the college are conducted bilingually (in English and Hindi), so that students, who find it difficult to understand English, can feel at home. Faculty seminars are conducted almost twice a month, where the faculty members of NTC, PTS, or sometimes guest professors present papers. In this regard, it is worth mentioning that NTC has good relations with other theological seminaries in the city, namely Doon Bible College and Presbyterian Theological Seminary.

Testimonies and Experiences of the Alumni of NTC from the Field:

Pastor K.P. Philipose, Arunachal Pradesh

After receiving Jesus Christ as my personal Savior and Lord in 1990, in Kerala, I came for the first time to Arunachal Pradesh with my aunty Achamma Philip. Through the born-again brothers at Arunachal, I came to know about the ministry of the Lord at Nagrakata, Jalpaiguri District, where Pastor Alex Jacob was ministering. I went to attend a crusade there in 1991. The main speakers were Uncle George and Rev. K.J. Kuriakose. They encouraged me to come and study the Word of God at NTC in a six-month discipleship course. I did not know any language other than my mother tongue, which is Malayalam, and there was a great fear in my heart as to how I would do full-time ministry. The six months that I spent at NTC changed my life. I used to spend 4-5 hours per day in prayer in my room at NTC that was a great blessing in my spiritual life, and I slowly learned to speak and read Hindi. Uncle George, Rev. K.J. Kuriakiose, and Rev. Simon Samuel played a very important role in the beginning years of my spiritual life and study at NTC. Uncle George's life and burden for India to be reached with the gospel touched my heart. I was gripped with a burden to reach out to the different tribes of Arunachal and to see the gospel preached and to plant churches all over this state.

For the first eight years of my ministry, I spent most of the time seeking the Lord through prayer and fasting. There were only a few families from South India in the Church at that time. My prayer to God was that God should enable me to preach the gospel and plant churches in every village and district of Arunachal Pradesh. In April 2001, after three days of fasting and prayer, there was a powerful move of the Holy Spirit. All of the people gathered for the meeting were filled with the Holy Spirit and spoke in tongues. The sick were healed and we witnessed many miracles. One lady from the Apatani tribe came for prayer, as she was suffering from a tumor in her stomach, and she was healed. A family from the Nishi tribe, under the power of witchcraft, received complete deliverance, and another man with kidney stones was miraculously healed. Additionally, an eighteen-year-old girl who was born blind received her sight. Many such miracles followed and the Lord sent a great revival in our midst.

The news of these miracles spread rapidly and soon people from different tribes, some who were officers, politicians, and ministers started visiting our church. People received Jesus as their personal Savior and were baptized. They were also filled with the Holy Spirit and started worshiping the Lord in Spirit and in truth. The people carried this good news to their respective villages. Then I, along with a few elders of the church, started visiting these villages to teach and preach the Word of God and slowly churches were established.

We felt the need to teach the Bible to these new believers and to train them, so we started conducting short Bible training programs, especially for the people in the interior regions. We organized 18 short courses, so we could equip and raise up evangelists for full time ministry. We also fasted and prayed as a church for 21 days, 14 days, and 7 days which helped break the strong evil forces in the land. People were set free from demonic and traditional types of bondage. The lifestyle of the people started to change, particularly their way of dressing, cooking, and conversation. Drinking and the selling of alcohol started decreasing, and today many villages have totally stopped selling alcohol.

Prayer has always been the backbone of the success of this ministry, and the women of our church are very dedicated and committed. We organized cottage prayer meetings, where believers gathered and prayed for a long time. Teaching the Word of God also has been an important part of this ministry. We have now ministered to 16 tribes and have established 40 churches in Arunachal and Assam. We have also had the opportunity to conduct prayer meetings in the house of the Chief Minister of Arunachal and also in the house of the Speaker and many other officers and politicians.

Arunachal is a land where no outsider can buy a piece of land and we need a permit to enter. I have had to struggle for my finances and in my personal life. My marriage was arranged by the NTC family and took place in Arunachal in the year 1994, but none of my family members attended my marriage. In the earlier days, in most places, the condition of the roads was terrible. I had to walk very long distances where no vehicle can go, and where there were no proper bathrooms and toilets, yet the Lord took care of me.

In 2009, I received threats from certain people to leave Arunachal and never return. One day I received a phone call threatening to cut off my hands and legs. Often I have faced discouragement in my life and even decided to quit the ministry at one point. We as a church also faced several attacks from the evil one. Many believers left the church, some have backslidden, and many of whom I had baptized left the church. This too caused great sorrow in my heart. But the Lord is restoring the Church and bringing new souls every day from all over Arunachal while opening new doors for ministry. Faithful is He who has called me, and He will do it. I will always confess along with Paul that I can do all things through Christ who strengthens me.

Santosh Lukose and Jessy Santosh

After completing our Bachelor of Divinity studies in New Theological College, we have been concentrating on reaching the unreached people in India with the gospel of Jesus Christ. Presently, we are running a Satellite Bible Training Center, named Jeevan Jyoti Institute of Communication (JJIC), situated in Nagpur, Maharashtra.

NTC has immensely influenced our lives for doing this ministry that we are now involved in. NTC increased our passion to bring the gospel to the unreached people in India, especially the passion of Uncle George for the need for more workers in the mission fields. During our study in NTC, we saw the importance of training for those who want to enter into the Lord's ministry. This allowed us to accept the responsibility of teaching in a Bible Training Centre when the authorities entrusted this job to us. The lives of our teachers at NTC have influenced us, especially in dealing with students and their issues. Our teachers were humble, friendly, and approachable. This influenced how we tried to instill these qualities in our own lives to help us in working with the students in JJIC. Particularly, our Principal, Dr. Simon Samuel's way of dealing with various issues related to students has been exemplary. We try to follow his footsteps in our lives as we deal with our students in JJIC.

Our responsibilities in JJIC includes teaching and the administration of the Training Center. I am also personally involved in giving leadership to the church-planting ministers in the Nagpur Team as well as coordinating the works of those who have graduated from JJIC (as per the directions of the state coordinator). JJIC is a Bible Training Institute engaged in giving one year training (in Hindi) to young people who desire to become church planters. The students are given free training (including free accommodation and food for the whole year). We have an average of 13 to 15 students a year. Most of them are sent by pastors of the CEA working in different villages of central India. Presently we are training our tenth class of students. Our students are tribal people mainly from the villages of Madhya Pradesh, Chhatisgarh, Uttar Pradesh and Maharashtra. Our vision includes planting as many churches as possible in Central India through the students we send out. So far, more than 100 young men have been sent out from JJIC.

We have seen very good results from the fields where our students pioneered churches. To our knowledge, more than 75% of the students sent out from JJIC are presently involved in church planting in various villages of Madhya Pradesh, Chhatisgarh, Uttar Pradesh and Maharashtra. Several of them are workers of the CEA, and some of them have more than one Church. In some churches, there are 100 or more members. Some of these church planters walk miles to reach their ministry fields due to a lack of conveyance. Some face oppositions from the villagers.

We are particularly delighted to see transformations and growth happening in the lives of our students. Brother S. Kumar, from Mandla district of Madhya Pradesh, was a recent convert freed from alcoholism. He was baptized in 2011, and came to JJIC for training soon after. Today, he is pastoring a church with more than hundred members. He sent three more students to study in JJIC in 2012, and another three in 2013. Another boy who used to chew "Tambakoo" (*local word for tobacco*) was sent by his parents to study at JJIC. He threw away his last sachet of Tambakoo when he reached the bus stop in Nagpur before entering the campus. Today, he is pastoring two churches with around thirty believers in Anuppur district of Madhya Pradesh. We usually have a special testimony session at the end of every academic year when students will share how JJIC has influenced their lives. One brother shared that he was a drunkard who could not live without alcohol when he was only 18 years of age. When he heard that his friend was coming to Nagpur (to JJIC) to study, he joined him even without having a personal experience of Christ. But after coming here, he came to know the Lord and became totally free from his addiction and became a transformed person.

In 2008, two illiterate students joined JJIC. One of them (like many of our other students) used to take care of cattle before coming here, but at the end of the year, during the Commissioning Service, both of these brothers received prizes for the best preaching and one of them scored the second highest mark in the examinations. Both of these brothers are now serving the Lord in Madhya Pradesh. Four years ago an orphan came to our Institute from Chennai, who had a vision to do ministry in North India. While in Chennai, he took a map of India in his hands and prayed to God for guidance, and he was directed to come to Nagpur, even though he could hardly speak Hindi. After coming to Nagpur, he began distributing Hindi tracts in the slums and came in contact with a pastor who knew JJIC. The pastor directed this brother to our Training Center, where he successfully completed the course (which is in Hindi), and scored the highest marks in the examinations that year. Presently, he is ministering in Manali, Himachal Pradesh.

Students often have very little knowledge of the Bible when they join JJIC. We mostly have students from Madhya Pradesh, Uttar Pradesh, Chhattisgarh, and Maharastra, who ministers of the CEA working in these places have sent to us. Most of these pastors go to more than one village to do their ministry. Many more villages still do not have even a single servant of God to minister to them. The pastors desire more trained ministers to do ministry in the villages where no one has started a ministry yet and to help the existing pastors. Some of these pastors themselves did not have any proper Biblical training. Such pastors earnestly hope that the students who complete their studies at JJIC will be able to help them in ministry, since they will come with more knowledge of the Bible. Often such pastors send suitable candidates back to JJIC from out of their own ministry. In the villages, people come to know Christ from being healed or because of deliverance from evil spirits. Many who come to JJIC do not even know who Christ is, or why Christ came to the world. Our responsibility starts at the ground level.

The socio-cultural backwardness of the students also poses a challenge. Most of our students come from very backward situations, with illiteracy, poor education, and lack of contact with urban life, addictions, and other bad habits. The students who come here are mostly from very remote parts of the country where the name of Jesus has never been heard. Most of them have never been to a city and some might never have travelled by bus. Their culture is extremely different, but it is our responsibility to love them, and sometimes even be like them so they might listen to us and trust us. There might even be cultural differences between different groups of students that can cause difficulties in adjusting to other students. It is our duty to make them feel at home even if we have to endure a lot of challenges in the process.

Many people ask us as to why we admit students with such backgrounds. Our answer to this question is that even if we have to endure a lot, we see transformation taking place in these students' lives during the training period and also see them develop a passion to serve and suffer for Christ. Another reason why we continue doing this ministry is because of the wonderful reports of our graduates that are reaching out to new people groups and planting churches. Because of these reports, we know that our labor is not in vain.

Pastor Sooraj Pal, Faculty of NTC.

The story of my encounter with Christ begins with a small piece of paper that I found lying in my wheat field while I was irrigating the field. It had the story of Jesus calming the storm while crossing the Sea of Galilee with the caption "Who is this Man?" I read the story with great eagerness and what impressed me was the power of Jesus over nature. However, this story about Jesus did not matter much to me, because this is a Christian story and I was a Hindu.

It was at this time one of my friends who was also my classmate in twelfth grade, shared the gospel of Jesus with me, and his own conversion story. More than his sharing, his humble and transformed life attracted me towards Christ. He called me to his home for a prayer meeting and there for the first time I heard the word of the Lord and felt in my spirit that this Jesus must be God. From that day onward, I started going to the church regularly, which was about fifteen kilometers from my village. The thought that Jesus died for my sins really touched me and I repented of all my sins. I felt the joy of the Lord in my heart as I became convinced that Jesus has now forgiven my sins. The Lord delivered me from all my sinful habits and gave me peace that I never experienced before. I also witnessed the Lord delivering many other people from various sicknesses, family problems and demon possession, which strengthened my faith in the Lord.

Trouble started when my family realized that every Sunday I was going to the Church. My brothers were very much against my new life style. They told me that we are Hindus, and therefore, I should stop going to Church. They did their best to stop me from moving in this new direction. They would often get angry and threaten me. Consequently, I started going to Church secretly. Church people were also not welcomed by my family members at home.

Things became even more difficult when my village, especially the village headman (*Pradhan*) came to know about my conversion to Christ. The village people threatened my family that if I continued in my new lifestyle, our family would be excommunicated from the village. Since I persisted in my new faith, the village headman called the *Village Panchayat* (Village Council of the Elders) to discuss the matter. The Village Council called my family and me, and the elders asked whether we had become Christians. My family denied that they were Christians. So the Council commanded us to bow down before the village god in the village temple, if we were not Christians. My whole family including myself bowed down before the idol that day and the council was dismissed. Even though no one asked me about my faith in Jesus in that Council, I was afraid because I could not confess my faith in Jesus and bowed down before the idol that day. I lost my joy and peace and for almost the whole night I kept crying thinking that Jesus would never receive me again because I had insulted him publicly. But the love and acceptance that I received from my church members again gave me the courage to get up and walk with Christ.

After a few months, once again a similar scenario arose. My family and I were called before the Village Panchayat and this time the Lord gave me courage to openly confess that I am a follower of Jesus and I would not forsake Christ at any cost. My eldest brother became so agitated at my confession that he got up before the Council and declared that if I did not forsake Christ, my family would have nothing more to do with me. With this discussion, the council was dismissed. Even though my family did not throw me out of the home after this incident, they were not good to me. Many times, I was mocked and insulted both by my family and the village people, but the word of the Lord and the fellowship of God's people encouraged me to continue in my new faith.

This went on for two years and my faith in Jesus grew. I was preparing to become a police officer and was working hard towards this goal. It was at this time while reading the word of the Lord, I felt the Lord calling me for his ministry. I was perplexed for sometime, but ultimately decided to serve the Lord. I consulted my pastor and other leaders and they advised me to go for the Bible training in Dehradun and thus began my academic pursuit in theology.

On 8th July 1996, I entered the campus of New Theological College (NTC), Dehradun. Ever since I heard about NTC through one of my friends, who was a student of the college at that time, I had a great eagerness and desire to come to Dehradun and study God's Word. But financial struggles and several other problems at home made me think that it was impossible for me to come to NTC. After many prayers and waiting upon the Lord, God opened the way for me to study, and I came to this school as an infant in Christ at a time when NTC itself was in its beginning stage.

I came to NTC with very little knowledge about Christ, but with great excitement to know God more. Christ to me was like the pearl that was costly, whom I desperately longed to know and to have. Indeed, I was not disappointed. NTC molded my life in Christ and taught me that life without Christ in this world is like a ship without radar. As an infant in Christ, I had my own apprehensions, struggles, and fears, which I underwent during my training period; but these experiences of life, became stepping-stones to greater spiritual depths, growth, and maturity in Christ.

Coming from a small village of Udham Singh Nagar of Uttarakhand, I was not only an infant in Christ but an infant in many other things, particularly with regard to my knowledge of the English language, various cultures and ethnic groups, and to a large extent of myself. NTC opened to me an avenue of vast knowledge and different experiences of life. NTC not only taught me theology, but also how to live with people of varied languages, cultures and ethnicity. NTC became my home where I started to grow up with brothers and sisters who belonged to different church backgrounds. At this time, even the idea of various churches and denominations was totally foreign to me, since I was a new convert and very new to Christianity.

Even though I had made fair progress in my studies, I experienced severe depression during the first two years of my studies in this place. As a result of that depression I often found myself unable to concentrate on my studies. But God's grace sustained me and carried me forward. I completed my B. Th. Degree in 2000 and joined NTC as a staff member. I was given the responsibility of leading the prayer ministry of the college, which I did with great enthusiasm since this has been my passion. In 2006, I completed my Bachelor of Divinity degree from NTC itself and started to teach as an assistant lecturer for a number of years and served as the chaplain of the college. Along with these ministerial responsibilities the Lord enabled me to undertake a MA degree in Organizational Leadership and Management, which I completed in 2012. In 2014 the Lord helped me to complete my Masters in Theology in the field of New Testament from Nav Jyoti Post Graduate and Research Center (NJPGRC) Delhi/Dehardun, of which NTC is a partner institution.

In 1996, the year I joined NTC as a student, I got the opportunity to serve leprosy patients who are despised and rejected by society. The colony, where these despised people lived, is situated at the outskirts of Dehradun city, about eight kilometers from NTC. Ministry among these people, along with my theological studies kept me in touch with the harsh realities of life and helped me to remain focused on the Lord. The love of Christ compelled me to serve these people with all of my heart and in return the love and affection that I received from these people gave me enough motivation to continue to serve them. After my marriage in 2002, my wife Preeti and I started living among these people and served them while continuing to work and study at NTC. Today our Church is growing among these people and has become a place of restoration and inner healing for many. In addition to this, God has enabled us to give leadership to two different churches that serve the Dalit and tribal communities in my native place. God has blessed my extended family and many of my family members and relatives have opened their hearts for Jesus and some of them are part of these growing churches.

I want to praise God for NTC and its contributions in my life. Humanly speaking what I am today is because of what NTC has contributed in my life. This is a place where I have grown up from infancy to adulthood. I have also seen NTC growing under the leadership of committed leaders and teachers and producing great leaders and scholars to serve the Lord in the Indian sub-continent. God has also enabled NTC to have wonderful facilities and a great infrastructure. Truly the hand of the Lord almighty is upon NTC and its various ministries. Presently, I am serving this institution as a lecturer, chaplain, prayer coordinator and also as a senior pastor of the above-mentioned church. My wife serves in the academic office of the College. We are so thankful to God for making us a part of this wonderful community. May God Almighty continue to bless and use NTC for His Kingdom and Glory.

Practices

NTC is committed to provide excellent training for grass-root level Christian workers and first generation Christians in advanced Christian leadership. Very soon after beginning ministerial training, BSS began to realize the need to establish schools for children in difficult areas in this hilly region and provide quality education for the children of poor laborers and unemployed people. BSS has established good schools that are committed to provide quality education. Quality primary and secondary education is an important need that exists in communities particularly in North India. Jesus loved children and blessed them, and children deserve an opportunity to study. They need to be treated as human beings with dignity and respect, who are created in God's image. The only possibility to redeem children from the utter poverty in which they are trapped is by providing them excellent education. BSS is currently supporting, fully or partially, ten primary/secondary schools that serve over 3,000 needy children. These schools, run by BSS, provide these children free tuition, clothes, books, periodic medical checkups, and one filling meal a day.

The Institute of Languages and Linguistics is the latest addition to the commitment and concern of BSS. This project develops mother-tongue translators through the Institute of Languages and Linguistics. This program trains missionaries in the area of professional competence necessary for their involvement as cross-cultural workers specializing in translation and literacy projects. Training is also offered in the national language and some state languages to train mother-tongue translators.

BSS has also expressed its concern for the poor and destitute by establishing orphanages and child care centers. A number of children are orphans and do not have parents to care for them. There are others whose parents are incapable of taking care of them. BSS realized the significance of establishing orphanages and childcare centers because there is a huge demand to cater to the need of such children. BSS intentionally keeps the number of children in each home at a restricted level so that each child can receive the best care possible. The goal is to provide each child holistic care that gives care for body, soul, spirit, and mind. The intention behind providing the best education possible for these children is to help them grow to be productive citizens of this country. As years have gone by, BSS expanded to care for the needy by providing counseling and medical care for poor pregnant mothers and providing relief and rehabilitation to poor people, whenever natural calamities took place in the state of Uttarakhand and sometimes helping other states as well. For example, during the *tsunami*, BSS collaborated with the Emmanuel Hospital Association to rebuild disaster-affected areas.

BSS is also interested in a church-planting ministry, guided by the most important commandments of our Lord Jesus. The most important commandment of Jesus is the call to love the Lord our God with all our heart, and with all our soul, with all our mind, and with all our strength. The second command of Jesus is to love our neighbor as ourselves. Jesus emphasized that there are no greater commandments than these two. BSS has taken the challenge to obey what Jesus taught. Through these schools and projects the BSS community expresses its love for God with all their heart, soul, mind, and strength. Through the church-planting ministries many lives have been transformed and many social evils have been eliminated. No one is compelled to respond to the call of Jesus that the Church proclaims. Everyone is free to have their own opinion with regard to the need for change in one's own personal life as well as social life.

LEARNINGS

From the beginning, it was the founder's passion to train men and women for diverse ministries in North India. He wanted to reach the unreached with the gospel of Christ through these ministries and believed that we can serve God only by loving and serving our brothers and sisters.

Uncle George believes in Christian leadership that is marked with an attitude to serve others in humility. He is committed to groom leaders who give priority to intelligence and integrity, spiritual fervor, and moral credibility. He believes in training leaders who have a heart for missions. For Uncle George, truth, integrity, and purity are not optional as one tries to live as a Christian and a true follower of Christ. These are of ultimate importance in order that we are known as children of God. A Christian leader is not only the one who preaches, but also one who seeks earnestly to practice Christian ideals in living out his/her personal and ministerial commitments. Uncle George believes that if new Christian ministries emerge with a strong sense of accountability and are willing to serve the church at large, then many such new Christian ministries are welcome. However, he hesitates to approve Christian ministries that are simply intended to duplicate others for the sake of personal profit. He cautions that in Christian ministry if personal gain or competitive spirit is at work, then there is a serious question concerning the genuine nature of the commitment. Therefore, it is of paramount significance to enter into Christian ministry with right motives and intentions. Beginning a Christian work with dubious, competitive, or ulterior motives cannot be the will of God. Subsequently, there is a need to raise Christian leaders who have a good character and attitude.

Uncle George also emphasizes that the Bible is the inspired Word of God. The writers were inspired by the Holy Spirit (2 Pet 1:21), and consequently the writings are inspired by God (2 Tim 3:16). The Bible is therefore a helpful tool in guiding a Christian to receive salvation that is available through faith in Christ. The Bible is also sufficient in matters regarding doctrine, correction, moral and ethical instruction (2 Tim 3:15-17). He always points out that the Bible reveals God's divine commands and principles regarding the way we ought to live, and so he often asks the students to read one Proverb a day and exhorts from each chapter at the beginning of the academic year. He teaches the students how to live our life as faithful and honest Christians. He challenges everyone to have a genuine faith in Christ that will transform our lives and minds. Subsequently, this transformation will lead us to a greater submission to the will of God. He ascertains that Biblical instruction gives sufficient guidance to perceive the will of God concerning how we should live, think, and interact with one another.

Uncle George stresses the importance of having a personal experience of Christ. This experience has a consequence. Our ability to understand the Holy Scripture is shaped in part by our personal experiences and the traditions that have shaped us. However, he categorically instructs that reason, tradition, and experience should be subservient to the Holy Scripture. They should not and cannot contradict biblical authority. Uncle is open to embrace Christians who belong to different traditions. He confidently teaches his understanding of the Bible, but also respects those who submit to biblical authority in different ways.

Training quality leaders and ministers has become the aim and highest goal of both BSS and NTC. Uncle George is offended by the fact that the life style of Christians today is not much different from the people of other faiths. Many Christians justify their worldly sins. Some theologians even criticize the call for holiness and argue that we should not be legalistic. However, obedience to the call to be the "New Creation" does not lead to pride or self-righteousness. The root, stem, leaves, and fruit of being the "New Creation" are founded on the love of God in Christ Jesus. He insists that we should be people who obey God's Word and avoid the dangers of legalism and unholy living.

Uncle George, in one of his articles, refers to Romans 8:29 and states that the Holy Bible demands that we Christians must be Christ-like. The eternal plan of God is to invite those who are redeemed by the work of Christ to be conformed to the likeness of His Son. The challenge before every Christian is to immerse oneself in the Word of God and the Holy Spirit. He writes, "We must immerse ourselves in the Word of God and the Holy Spirit. Both the Word and the Spirit must be allowed to work in our lives in such a way that every nook and corner of our life is 'soaked' with the Word and the Spirit. Nothing must be allowed to remain as old. 'Christ-likeness' is such a total transformation. It is indeed radical." This foundational belief has led the leaders of NTC to form strict rules and regulations for the students of NTC to follow.

The challenge was to win the confidence of the rural communities through our BSS staff. Even though the early leaders of this movement had to face caste discriminations, illiteracy, and the social and economic backwardness of these rural communities, they did not give up. The first task cut out for the BSS movement was to bring awareness among these communities about development and social work. According to the visionaries of BSS, it was the combination of social work and church planting work that can provide the impetus to bring about holistic development in these communities. An additional advantage of this ministry is that the BSS staff members are theologically trained, and a strong theological understanding of mission is essential to positively penetrate the lives of rural people to bring development and change. The strong theological viewpoints of the movement help the people to integrate truths about God with everyday practical life. This is the inner force that propels the movement through difficult times. However, it took almost 25 years to build this rural community to a point to face their socio-cultural and economic challenges with the spirit of Christ.

Our ministries provide a platform for the poor people of this region to express themselves in the midst of ongoing oppression. Different groups of people belonging to this section of society are brought together under one umbrella. They have embraced a new identity through the work of BSS, and their children study together in our schools. We are able to address some basic issues such as health awareness and income generation, plus we are able to help them in the process of human development as well as infrastructure development in a small way in their communities. Today, the people in these communities have learned to save resources for their future generations. So, we can confidently say that those who have embraced this mission movement have progressed in their life situation socially, economically and spiritually. Through BSS projects and schools, we continue to mold and groom the present generation based on the principles of Biblical truth.

Now the ministry has grown to such an extent that it can deal with the problems of society along with its involvement in developmental works and in the area of education. As a result, literacy levels have increased in these communities. The schools have not only provided a platform to serve such communities, but they also gave BSS credibility and respect among the local people. Subsequently, BSS workers become a part of these communities. BSS workers have addressed the issues of the caste system, and have brought the Dalits, Garhwalis, and other "outcast" people under one roof, by allowing their children to study together in BSS schools. Second, this movement impacted the economic development of these communities. The "income generating" programs and self-help groups started by the Jeevan Jyoti Bal-Vikas led families to become self-reliant and set them on the path of economic development.

BSS strongly believes that education is not merely about imparting knowledge. Therefore, conscious attempts are always made to turn schools into temples of learning where character is built, minds are inspired, talents are nurtured and values are imbibed. These schools have been really successful in imparting biblical values to children and molding them to be responsible citizens with high moral and ethical values. These schools have the vision to see the future of India in the hands of such citizens who have received value-based education based on the teachings of our Lord Jesus Christ. A committed ministerial team of young men and women who have committed themselves to serve God by serving people runs the BSS schools. Most of them are theologically trained from New Theological College. These young men and women are actively serving in these schools as well as in the local churches. God has used the school leadership and ministerial teams to establish churches in this region and to give spiritual nurture to the believers in these new churches.

The founder of BSS and NTC emphasized the spreading of the good news, when he wrote, "We have found the greatest treasure in the world. We must not keep it for ourselves. We cannot delay the good news we have received and experienced. 'This day is a day of good news, but if we are keeping silent; if we wait until morning light, punishment will overtake us (2 Kings 7:9).'" Uncle George quoting from II Kings, particularly referring to the experience of the lepers, asserts that if we withhold the most wonderful good news for just ourselves, God will hold us accountable.

FUTURE

People who oppose this movement in these villages try to raise their voice against the socio-economic development by accusing us of converting these people to Christianity and by threatening them with exclusion from the society. They try to stop the spiritual growth of these poor people by intimidating them with the help of police and other government machinery. Such opposition is likely to continue.

The Dalit community has to take up political challenges on their own. The awareness and income generation programs help the community to fight against exploitation and marginalization. However, the political issues are still not addressed. The Dalit community is still deprived of their right to the land where they have lived for many years. The BSS movement needs to be involved in such issues in the future in order to build the Kingdom of God further among these people.

School as a secular institution needs to keep its credibility in society. At the same time, we are appointing and promoting theologically trained men and women to join this mission. The challenge is to maintain professionalism in the educational sector and still do effective mission work simultaneously. The church-planting ministry could be affected if the pressure of the school ministry increases. However, as a team, we are trying our level best to bring both aspects of ministry together in close proximity. We need more clarity on this issue and need to evolve a methodology that can help us in leading the church and at the same time help us to be professionally qualified teachers for our students. NTC is able to partially address this issue through the double degree program.

The level of enthusiasm of the BSS staff can be variable. Often, when expectations are not met, there are some who drop out over time. But it is very important to note that many are improving in their commitment and growing very fast in maturity in ministry and accomplishing much. One of the reasons for this variation in enthusiasm could be the proper placement of people according to their level of interest. If people can be properly placed in the various responsibilities according to their ability and interest in a more effective way, it will help them perform and contribute more to the growth of this ministry.

The Uttarakhand government has declared areas where we work as an industrial area, and consequently many industries were established in this area. Big industrial units were built on agricultural lands. So many families were displaced and lost their livelihood. Many of these agricultural laborers lost their jobs and joined these industrial units as daily wage laborers. Almost all of the parents of our school/project children in this area work in these private industries as daily laborers for meager daily wages. They are not professionally and educationally trained to handle the technical jobs in these industries, as most of them are illiterate. For this reason, people from outside of the area are coming and taking the important jobs, depriving local people of economic development. Such larger economic trends need to be addressed by the churches.

The community as a whole faces many kinds of discrimination in various dimensions of life such as the test of their competence level while seeking employment in a company as well as in their daily work as agricultural laborers. In the area of employment, these simple poor village people are discriminated against and exploited by these industries that deprive them of their legitimate profit. Secondly, their agricultural land is taken away by the owners of the industries to start even bigger industries and have left these people landless and jobless. This discrimination eventually marginalized their children and their families and has pushed them into the corner of economic poverty. However, our schools and projects have taken the risk to address some of these issues. Lately, we have started a computer center for the education of the children of one community and with the help of "Self Help Groups" we are able to conduct many awareness programs seeking the welfare of the community as a whole. More focused economic issues need to be met by innovative ministries on the local level.

Even though the schools and the projects have been successful in obeying the divine mandate, there have been several challenges along the way. Lack of financial resources and scarcity of committed and qualified staff to teach in the schools in remote places, are just a few examples that have been real challenges that we continue to face. But God has been faithful, and He has honored the vision and commitment of BSS founding fathers and mothers and all the past faithful co-workers of BSS. The challenge in the future will be to be faithful to the divine mandate and the motto of our schools to "teach everyone in all wisdom", and to serve the nation of India by providing the best value-based education that can lead to social and spiritual transformation. We must strive to avoid the pitfall of becoming too bureaucratic and to maintain cordiality. The BSS and NTC communities have to believe that they are one big family. The founding fathers and mothers intended and still insist that this community should function like a family, even though these ministries have now become established institutions.

Uncle George remarked, "If we open our eyes and look, we will see that hundreds within the 4693 people groups of India are still without a witness. Forty-five of the largest 100 unreached people groups in the world are in India. We still have scores of languages without even a portion of the Word of God. Do we see any of these? Do we care? Or are we so preoccupied by our silly church politics and narrow minded parochialism that we have neither time, nor energy, nor resources for millions who still live in darkness?"

Uncle George writing on the theme: *Bringing in the Sheaves* (Psalm 126:6) asserts that we have the test cut out for us; we need to bring life and hope by proclaiming that there is abundant life in Christ. Christ came to give abundant life to all who open their hearts to him. "We must proclaim this good news to every one of our brothers and sisters in India ... If we obey the Master (Matthew 9:38) with all of our hearts, we will see a harvest in India like none of us is expecting."

As responsible citizens, Christians must help India in overcoming many social evils such as illiteracy, slave labor, child labor, child marriage, abortion, infanticide of baby girls, corruption, false gurus who mislead people, and religious militants. Uncle George writes, "Every Christian has a sacred responsibility to work hard to bring as much freedom as possible to each and every one of our brothers and sisters. We must not idly stand by allowing our mother India to suffer any form of bondage. Jesus spoke of true freedom that comes only from knowing Him. India desperately needs this freedom."

As a revitalization movement, BSS and NTC impart new traits in Christian ministries that are not found in other seminaries and institutions. There is a positive chain reaction from the founder to the co-workers and students involved in this ministry. The leader's vision is unique and special. His vision is founded on perceiving reality and God's concern in a new and fresh way, even though it involves huge commitment and sacrifice. Uncle George as the leader of this organization is always ready to share his experiences in the beginning and even now as to how God is at work in this ministry. He is truly a visionary who has a clear-cut understanding of what his co-workers and those who want to be trained here should be and ought to become. The founder imparts love and has an understanding spirit and beckons all his coworkers to cooperate with each other in fulfilling God's plans and purposes for this generation through this ministry. The founder is one who deeply trusts God to overcome every phase of conflict and resistance by trusting in the call, commission, and confirmation that he received from God to reach the unreached people groups with the gospel of Christ in this generation.

Case Study Two: The Christian Evangelistic Assemblies (CEA)

VARGHESE SAMUEL

84 | CASE STUDY TWO: THE CHRISTIAN EVANGELISTIC ASSEMBLIES

Abstract: The Christian Evangelistic Assemblies (CEA) is a North India based church-planting ministry started in 1987. It was registered with the Government of India as a charitable society in 1994, though it functions as a church. It is an individually initiated church, but charismatically driven and functions with a formal administrative structure and has a presence in most of the North Indian states and Nepal. CEA's focus is on establishing churches in places where there are no churches. It has the largest number of churches in Orissa and probably the biggest church in Arunachal Pradesh. It has churches both in urban and rural contexts. In terms of its growth and spread, CEA can be seen as a Christian renewal movement. The Christian Evangelistic Assemblies is a fellowship of evangelical charismatic churches committed to the cause of the gospel of Jesus Christ in fulfilling the Great Commission by taking the gospel to every tribe, language, and people and to plant indigenous worshiping congregations. Its mission is not limited to bringing spiritual change in the lives of people, but also to cause visible and tangible changes in social, intellectual, and economic areas and above all bring personal transformation, which will result in a larger holistic transformation of the community.

DEFINITION

Rev. Dr. George and Leela Chavanikamannil founded the Christian Evangelistic Assemblies and dedicated their lives for the propagation of the gospel in North India. Their passion is to see churches planted among as many unreached people groups as possible. Early on they realized that the task is too large for any one person or group to achieve. In 1984, while serving the Lord with World Vision International, George had a special experience with God. The Lord had called him for ministry in North India in 1967. He was making all kinds of excuses to escape from the call. One excuse was that it was useless for him to go to North India because the task was way too big for him. As if to prove his point with God he decided to "show it to God with the aid of an adding machine." He imagined the following scenario. "Suppose he goes back to North India and starts preaching to one thousand different persons a day. How long will it take to evangelize 800 million people, then the population of India?" The answer he got with the aid of the adding machine shocked him. "2,191.78 years!" Though he knew the task was huge, he had no idea that it was that huge. While being totally discouraged and trying to convince God to leave him alone, the Holy Spirit gently told him that if there were

2,191.78 people doing it, it would take only 1 year to achieve the goal! (By the way, if the same scenario were played out today it would take 2,739.72 years to reach a billion people. India has nearly 1.3 billion people today.)[37]

For the first time in his life George felt that he was beginning to understand the seriousness of the words of our Lord in Matthew 9:37: "The harvest is plenteous but the laborers are few ..." Slowly the Lord instilled in him and Leela the vision to do everything they possibly could to train laborers and help them to go to unreached places and peoples.

Soon they learned that North India is home to the largest number of unreached people groups ("nations") in the world. Of the 4,693 people groups or *jathi* of India hundreds have no witness at all. Most Indian languages translate the New Testament Greek word *ethna*, that is used in the Great Commission passages and translated as *"nations"* in English, by the word *jathi*. (According to the Anthropological Survey of India, the country has 4,693 *jathi*.) The Lord's command to His Church is to make disciples of all "*jathi*" or nations (Matthew 28: 19-20). Most unreached nations in India are in the North. This motivated George and Leela to locate the ministry in North India and not their own native South.

But how can such large numbers of *jathi/nations* be reached with the Gospel? Many of these people groups are resistant to even Indians who do not belong to their own communities, not to mention foreigners. (India has effectively shut its door to Western missionaries in 1975 and thus the Church in India can no longer depend on missionaries from outside to fulfill the Great Commission). So the only practical way to accomplish the task is by training and supporting as many *native missionaries* as possible. This became the central part of their vision.

"As a primary step into the ministry in North India, George founded Bharat Susamachar Samiti (BSS) in Dehra Dun, in North India in 1986. Under this parent body, Luther W. New Jr. Theological College, popularly known as New Theological College was founded in 1987."[38] The training of ministers started in 1987, when many students from different states and tribes of India joined the short-term courses in the early years of the college. As the students received training they also

---

37 Interview with Rev. Dr. George Chavanikamannil, Founder of Christian Evangelistic Assemblies.
38 P.V. Joseph, A North Indian Mission Paradigm: Life and Vision of George Chavanikamannil, Beginnings, Dehra Dun:NTC, 2012, pg. 26.

were challenged to take the gospel to the unreached places in India. Consequently, several of them ventured into semi-urban and rural areas and planted small congregations. Pastors of these congregations came together for fellowship and prayer and attracted a few likeminded pastors who joined the fellowship. As the number of fellowship gatherings grew and spread through different nearby states, it became necessary to have a formal organization of churches to function well and to fulfill the vision and mission of the founder. "… ministries were started in a few places in three states of India, (Uttar Pradesh, Madhya Pradesh and Orissa) and a few congregations were established. It was in 1992, the ministry was formalized and Christian Evangelistic Assemblies was officially formed."[39]

The founder, Rev. Dr. George Chavanikamannil, along with a few leaders who were working with him at that time, called the first meeting of the leaders of Christian Evangelistic Assemblies. The first meeting of the Board of Directors of Christian Evangelistic Assemblies[40] was held on Tuesday, the 19th of June 1992 on the premises of New Theological College. In this meeting, important decisions were taken as to the future direction, functioning, and structure of the church. Some of the decisions that actually shaped the course of action to achieve the vision and goals of the organization[41] included: the decision to expand to all the states of India with national registration, to work in teams going to new places where the gospel had not been preached, and to appoint ministers at three different levels (recognized, licensed, and ordained). Thus the informal ministry took on the form of an organized church. These decisions provided enough enthusiasm to encourage the members to press on towards the goal. Yet, much work remained to be done.

The CEA realized the need to train and equip young men and women to work in the villages and towns in North India. Several young men and women had been trained in New Theological College, and depending on the need and complexity of the ministry, they were trained either for one year or for four years. Many of them have now gone to other places and established churches.[42]

---

39 Varghese Samuel, Christian Evangelistic Assemblies: Celebrating God's Faithfulness for 20 years, Niyog 2011, Dehra Dun: NTC, 2011, pg. 29.
40 Minutes of the Board of Governors of the Christian Evangelistic Assemblies, June 19, 1992.
41 Minutes of the Board of Governors of the Christian Evangelistic Assemblies, June 19, 1992.
42 Varghese Samuel, 'Christian Evangelistic Assemblies: Celebrating God's faithfulness for 20 years', Niyog 2011, Dehra Dun:NTC, 2011, pg. 30.

As the ministry expanded to cover more than ten Indian states, it became necessary to further organize the ministry's structure to be more effective. Hence, the churches in different states were brought under regional organizations. In 1993, the ministry was segregated into three regions – the Northern, North Eastern and Central regions. Later these regions were further expanded to include seven additional regions: 1. Arunachal & Assam, 2. Bihar & Jharkhand, 3. Orissa & Andhra Pradesh, 4. Madhya Pradesh, Maharashtra & Chhattisgarh, 5. Delhi & Haryana, 6. Uttar Pradesh & Uttarakhand, 7. Punjab and Himachal Pradesh, and coordinators were assigned to oversee these ministries and meet with the pastors regularly once in a month.[43]

To make the work even better coordinated and more effective, the ministers in every team gather together every month to discuss strategy, to pray together, to listen to others and to have fellowship. It is mandatory for every minister to be part of a team, as it was found that members of a team performed better than those who worked independently. The reason is that they receive better support, guidance, and necessary help in times of need. Rev. Mathews Varghese served as the National Coordinator from 1994 to 2012, coordinating the ministries travelling to all the churches, and his contribution has helped the ministry to grow considerably.

CONTEXT

The vision of the CEA is to preach the Gospel and plant churches in as many unreached places and among as many unreached people groups in the Indian subcontinent as possible. We desire to see societies transformed by the grace of our Lord Jesus Christ through His Church. How can this vision become a reality? As illustrated earlier, the founders realized that no one could accomplish this alone. The reality described by Lord Jesus in Matthew 9:37 was taken seriously. It was clearly understood that unless well-trained, committed laborers are there in plenty, the vision would never be fulfilled. So the first and most strategic step in the mission was to train new laborers with the same vision and recruit those who shared the vision and then send them to unreached people groups and places. Thus the CEA's mission first focused on this two-prong approach- a) train AND recruit men and women with the same vision of reaching the unreached and, b) send them and support them to plant churches in unreached places and among unreached people groups. The recruiting of like-minded people, sending them and

---

43 Niyog 2011, pg. 30.

supporting them began in 1987. Training of new workers began in 1989 through New Theological College.

From the beginning the CEA has been challenged by the words of James 2: 15-16: "Suppose a brother or sister is without clothes and daily food. If one of you says to him, 'Go, I wish you well; keep warm and well fed,' but does nothing about his physical needs, what good is it?" (NIV). While preaching the Gospel and making disciples is our supreme priority, we cannot close our eyes to pressing human needs. Holistic transformation requires holistic approach to human needs. The aims and objectives for which the CEA is established include:[44] teaching the truth of scripture, providing education (formal and informal), vocational training, medical care, support for orphans, widows, the aged, and needy, the construction and maintenance of church structures, and to promote fellowship among believers and understanding among the different sections of society.

The Christian Evangelistic Assemblies aim to make its churches self-sufficient, as much as possible. Indian churches have been criticized through the centuries for being dependent on help and support from Western churches and missions. This is partially true because of the evangelism strategy of Western missionaries. The missionaries found that the most receptive groups to the gospel were the underprivileged caste groups who were socially and economically deprived, and as a result highly dependent on the upper caste for their sustenance. [45]Converts from these groups were often dependent on the missionaries, even after their conversion to Christianity. The missionaries continued to help the converts to keep their allegiance and support, although this mission culture kept the new converts dependant. The missionaries did this with good intentions; however, it made Indian Christians and the Indian Church heavily dependent on Western funds.

After the departure of Western missions and missionaries, the church in India went through a period of stagnancy, even deterioration. Once the inflow of funds stopped, pastors and believers who were heavily dependent on Western sources were perplexed as to how to continue to sustain the church. Bewildered leaders started selling properties. This phenomenon is seen mainly in the mainline churches where the growth of Christian members is less than in new emerging churches. With the help of global missions and mission-minded churches in the

---

44 Memorandum of Association, Christian Evangelistic Assemblies, pg. 2.
45 Robert Reese, Western Missions and Dependency, http://www.wmausa.org/page.aspx?id=289947.

West and elsewhere, there emerged a number of churches that came to be known as evangelical charismatic churches. We perceive the CEA as one such church. As the political scenario and statutory regulations change, the Indian church will find it difficult to continue depending on the West. Hence the church has to find sources within India. One of the primary goals of the CEA is to make its churches self-sufficient.

DEVELOPMENT

Bhopal - Good News Church and Center (GNCC)

Rev. Mathews Varghese and his wife Daisy initiated this ministry in a leading city where less than 1% of the total population is Christian. Having received a call and vision, they moved to Bhopal in 1987 with a conviction to plant churches. Several people were trained and joined the team and the ministry has expanded to the surrounding areas. Other supporting ministries and activities include church planting (including Sehore, Ayodhya Nagar, Mandeedeep, Bagmugalia, Gandhi Nagar, Nehru Nagar, Indore and several places in the district of Mandala and the state of Chhattisgarh). In addition, with the aim to equip young people who want to enter in full time ministry, GNCC provides a two-year training program in discipleship and ministry. Every year 20-25 men and women are trained, who then go to places where the gospel is not preached.

Jeevan Jyoti School at village Tarsevaniya contributes by educating 250 children in the area surrounding Bhopal. The school was started in 1992, and presently there are classes up to grade eight. The school serves as a springboard for children from economically poor backgrounds to achieve a better education. In addition, with the aim to help street kids, GNCC has started two programs. 1. *Anmol Kids* was started in 2006 with the aim to help rag picker children. In four slums 300 children are gathered every week and they are cleaned, fed, given necessary supplies, taught and counseled. 2. *Saharakiran* is a hostel started in 2008 for poor and orphaned children; currently fifteen children are being cared for in this hostel. They are given necessities and also attend school.

Other projects seek to empower the poor. There is a project to train and empower women from economically poor backgrounds, especially slum dwellers, to help them acquire skilled vocational training and literacy. The women are taught to read and write, and the skill of tailoring. These centers are called *Anugraha Tailoring Centers*. The program was started in 2002 and presently there are 13 such training centers. A total of 2082 women were trained here. In addition, once a week the church goes out to a poor area where people are in need of food and the church provides 200 food packets.

The village school has proved to be a strong means of Christian testimony in several villages through which the rural folk know about Christian values. So far, more than 200 students completed grade eight from this school, and many of these students were able to continue their education in other places, and have been placed in good positions in their present careers. In the area of education, this school has had a major impact and today there is not a family left without someone who is literate. There is an increasing interest among the girls in the villages for education, and the first female graduate from this village completed her primary school education in our school.

The influence of the church in the spiritual realm cannot be neglected. The members of the churches, staff, and volunteer workers are involved in spiritual warfare to stand against the powers of satanic forces that are prevailing in this region. We believe that tremendous changes have taken place in the development of the city and in its social, educational, economic, and cultural areas. This ministry is an agent of change.

Delhi

Christian Evangelistic Assemblies started its ministry in Delhi when it was registered in 1994. However, the ministry picked up momentum in 1997. It was a small beginning with Pastor John Prakash Kalathil, Pastor Saju Varghese, and Brother Wilson Das. These brothers have worked for a few years and started small congregations. But, in 2005, the ministry was more formally organized, and Pastor John Varghese and a few other young ministers took the challenge of reaching out to the needy and the unreached among the lower and middle class people. Delhi already had many churches, but most of the churches were either mainline churches or churches among middle class people. The church needed to reach out to the unreached lower class and lower middle class people as well. The CEA is focusing its ministry among the lower and/or middle class people of the society in Delhi.

The church-planting ministry began by door-to-door evangelism, personal evangelism and public meetings in various localities. Families going through various problems like sickness, satanic influence, alcohol/drug addiction and various other problems began to respond. It has been shown that miracles are key to relating the gospel to people and their needs. Unless signs and wonders take place, conversion or repentance does not often take place.

The CEA has its headquarters (registered office) in East Delhi, and since an office is already in place – a ministry also started here. Churches have also been planted in Khicripur/Kalyanpuri, Nandnagari (includes miracles of deliverance and feeding poor children and the elderly once a month), and in North Delhi in Jehangirpuri (work in a slum area started in 2000).

Although this is rather a small area of CEA involvement, we have stories of men delivered from alcohol use, young men delivered from addiction of drugs, husbands and wives on the verge of divorce reunited after counseling by the pastor, and families contemplating suicide because of huge debts who changed their mind and decided to live because they found peace and joy in Christ. One example of this is Om Prakash, an auto rickshaw driver who had incurred a huge debt over time and had no way of paying the money back. The moneylender threatened him many times, and although he sought help from many people, nobody was willing to hear his plea to the point that he was contemplating suicide. As a last resort he decided to go to a CEA church, where he heard about a God who gives peace and helps when everyone else abandons us. He believed in Jesus Christ, and the pastor counseled him and advised him about having discipline in his life and how to save money. In one year he had settled all his debts, and in the following year he bought a rickshaw of his own. We have seen families being transformed and then becoming building blocks to a better society. The impact on the society as a whole is yet to be seen, but is very visible in the church.

Literacy is something the church has learned to focus on. There are many sisters in our church who did not even know how to read or write before coming to church. A sister named Seema along with her husband started coming to church. After her husband passed away, she was given a Bible to read and she told us that she could not remember going to school as a child. Now after 3 years, she can read the Bible fluently. Girls are often compelled to leave school at a young age. We have learned to stand with these young girls and compel their parents to continue giving them an education. The church has encouraged and helped many children who have dropped out of school to go back and study.

Bihar

Nand Kumar, a local convert from Hinduism, is the pioneer of the CEA ministries in Bihar, which only recently started. Nand Kumar has the gifts of evangelism and healing, and many people are healed through his prayer. He also has a heart to minister to the needs of the people that help them to respond to the gospel. The nature of the CEA work here is evangelistic, with a focus on church planting, and training. Considerable progress has been made in a short period of time in all these areas. Brother Nand actually started to share his testimony of healing to other people which prompted them to seek healing from Jesus. A few people were healed in the initial days, which actually helped the ministry grow. The following testimony of a woman who was delivered from demon possession was also significant.

Laxmi (name changed) is an ordinary woman who lived in a village in the Lauki district of Bihar. She was possessed by a demon that gave her extra-ordinary strength. She would sleep in her home every night, but wake up somewhere else far from her home without knowing how she got there. Many times people also abused her. She would eat enough food for 5-6 people, yet she would stay very slim. Her family became very frustrated because they could not afford to keep her and provide for her. She had great strength when she was possessed, so that nobody could control her, but when she was not possessed she was very weak and frail. She was not afraid of a flooding river and she had the strength to swim against the force of the surging water because of the power of the demon. Because of the demon possession everyone was frustrated and worried. They took her to many witchdoctors and shamans, but even after many *pujas* and sacrifices, she was not delivered. Finally, as a last resort, she was brought for prayer to Brother Nand Kumar's church. The church prayed for her and she was delivered from the demon. This helped her family and others to trust in Jesus Christ and many people came to Christ as a result.

Testimonies of healing and deliverance from demon possession spread around by word of mouth and people started gathering from curiosity as well as to seek help. It is usually healing from physical ailments and deliverance from demonic forces that brought people to Jesus. They came to believe that Jesus is more powerful then the gods they have been worshipping. The main church now has more than 600 believers, and there are also several churches in the surrounding villages.

The gospel and the church have brought much change in the spiritual, social, economic, and educational realms. Believers who attend the church regularly have completely given up idol worship and Hindu festivals. But at a social level, that change is not very visible yet. Even women and children from an early age socially accept the use of alcohol and tobacco in this region. Christians are helping to deliver people from these addictions, as well as reducing the incidents of polygamy, polyandry, adultery and fornication, which are prevalent in Bihar. In addition, the church is helping to reduce the cases of child marriage through making a birth certificate mandatory before someone can marry.

The pastors are making a remarkable effort in bringing awareness about the importance of education to the people of Bihar. This has brought about a big difference, since Christian parents now want to send their children to school. Besides this, the pastors who have undergone one year of Bible training want to pursue their Biblical studies even further. However, there are no Christian schools here and often children are required to bow down and worship idols before school starts, and this deters many faithful Christians from sending children to school.

Uttarakhand (UK) and Uttar Pradesh (UP)

The Christian Evangelistic Assemblies had started its ministry in 1987 in Uttar Pradesh, the most populous state in India and a heavily Hindu area (80%). The ministry had been started by Rev. George Chavanikamannil to train young people for evangelism and church planting. As the graduates of the training center started establishing small congregations, a small fellowship came into existence. As the vision of the founders and the leaders was to take the gospel to unreached places, it was decided to venture into different places in UP and UK where churches do not exist. The ministry actually started in Dehra Dun and spread to neighboring places.

Pastor Reji John, a graduate of Doon Bible College, joined the ministry to reach out to Haridwar, the Hindu holy city. Reji started a primary school near Haridwar in 1990, and through the medium of the school, the gospel was shared to the students and to the people around the school. Almost at the same time Pastor

Daniel Masih, who is a native of Saharanpur, joined with a vision to reach out to the city. He along with a few others started to reach out to the society identifying the needy and ministering to them. People started responding, especially when divine and miraculous incidents happened, like healings and exorcisms. Later the graduates of New Theological College who were committed to minister in UP and Uttarakhand moved to different places, such as Jamunkhata, Poanta Sahib, Narendra Nagar, Raipur, Bhagawanpur, Pathri, Andheri, etc. and established churches. In establishing churches in and around Dehra Dun, the teachers and graduates of NTC had played a vital role in the growth of the Church.

In Uttarakhand and UP, the focus of the ministry was training and education. In Haridwar, Narendra Nagar, Bhagawanpur, and Jamunkhata, either schools or training centers were started, as it seemed most feasible. These places were considered as *dev bhoomi* (land of the gods) and the presence and propagation of other religions were not appreciated. Hence, schools were used as a means to reach out to the people. Schools gave acceptance and access among the people as everybody wanted their children to be educated. As a result, many churches were established in the areas around the schools. Many teachers also served as evangelists and missionaries. There were also training centers in Saharanpur, Narendra Nagar, Jamunkhata and Bareilly. These training centers played an important role in strengthening local believers with zeal and equipping them for evangelism.

In Western Uttarakhand, Dr. Sam Thomas and his medical team played a significant role in spreading the gospel and establishing churches. Dr. Sam worked in Herbert Christian Hospital as a surgeon, and at the same time he worked as an evangelist and pastor. He is also a pastor and leader of the CEA and shared the gospel with his patients at the clinic, visited them at home, and helped them in whatever way possible. He also conducted medical camps in villages where there were no medical facilities, and hundreds of people used to turn up for these camps. The gospel was preached, tracts and Bible portions were distributed, and people were prayed over at these events. The prayers of Dr. Sam healed patients who famous hospitals had given up on. Kehm Singh was one young man who lived in Singhpura village in Himachal Pradesh, who was converted along with his family while being treated and ultimately healed from Leukemia through Dr. Sam's work and prayers.

Medical facilities are expensive and not accessible for the poor. Many times people give up and accept their fate and succumb to suffering, but when the church offers them a way out through faith in Christ and prayer, they find a ray of hope. Many people have been healed miraculously, like Mona, a 19-year-old girl, a resident of Haridwar who was infected with a leprosy-like disease. Her skin, especially on the hands and feet, turned white and was bruised. She could not even breast feed her baby. She visited doctors in the government hospitals and their treatment did not help her. She was unable to go for further treatment in expensive private hospitals because her family could not afford it. Hearing her predicament, Pastor Reji John's wife and another sister visited her and shared the gospel. They also invited her for a fasting and prayer meeting in the school in Pathri. As Pastor Reji was sharing from the Word, filled by the Holy Spirit, he told Mona that the Lord was going to heal her and would testify about the healing on the following Sunday. They prayed over her and sent her home. Mona slowly started feeling better, and the next Sunday Mona came and showed her hands to everybody. The healing process had started. Slowly, she was completely healed. This was one of the first miracles to happen in Haridwar. The news spread to the villages and many people came for prayer and received healing.

There are examples of personal transformation also, as people were delivered from bad habits and evil life styles and became good citizens of the Kingdom as well as the country. Lalmani was a thug and a *dacoit*. He lived near a jungle and robbed people for a living. He and his gang stopped passing vehicles and robbed everything, threatening and beating those who resisted. For many years he was a nightmare for the people and the police. He was arrested several times and thrown into jail. However, when he came out of jail, he did the same thing. One day he happened to listen to the message of a Christian preacher who preached about the judgment of every person according their deeds and about heaven and hell. This convicted Lalmani and he decided to leave his way of life. He stopped robbing and gave all the possessions he earned by robbing to poor people and decided to follow Jesus. He became the disciple of a senior pastor and stayed with him for several years. He also attended a short Bible training course and became an evangelist.

The caste system is another dividing factor in most Indian communities. People are hesitant to mingle with people from other castes. Despite the teaching of all being one in Christ, people find it very difficult to associate with one another. However, the church has brought down the dividing wall to some extent. Though they are often unwilling to visit the houses of people from other castes, they come together for Christian worship. There is a feeling of belonging to a new community.

Being in Christ has also changed the living status of people. People who were living in poverty have started an upward movement in their lives. Earlier the men spent their money of alcohol, drugs, tobacco and on adultery, and the women had to work hard to make ends meet. Now, the money and effort they wasted on bad habits has been saved for the use of their family and the education of the children. There are hundreds of such testimonies. There is peace and joy in homes, as husbands and wives together make their lives and the lives of their children better. Also there is a greater awareness among people about the importance of education. Now they want to send their children to school, instead of the fields, and give them the good education that they were formerly deprived of.

In spite of all the positive changes that have happened in the lives of people, the church and the ministry has invited undue attention by anti-Christian religious fanatics. Many of them are jealous of the changes in the lives of people. Even more, they are disturbed by the increase of the number of Christians in the area. Fifteen years ago there was not even one Christian in a land that is considered to be a "land of the gods," but now there are hundreds, probably thousands of Christians. A kind of insecurity gripped them, a fear that they are losing ground that made them antagonistic to Christian activities. Several pastors have been summoned to the police stations and unnecessarily harassed and intimidated. Worship has been disturbed and stopped, worship places were vandalized, and Christian workers have been assaulted.

Orissa

The CEA started its work in Orissa, an area known for its antagonistic attitude toward Christians from the beginning, around 1987. A couple of ministers who joined the CEA at the start, Pastor I.D. Suna and Pastor Praveen Moni, were from Orissa and wanted to start a ministry there. I.D. Suna began his ministry in Koraput district and a group of enthusiastic young people joined him. This actually brought a revival to the area, and many people responded to the gospel and several churches were established. Pastor Praveen Moni started his ministry in Sundargarh district in eastern Orissa, others joined him later and the ministry grew in different parts of the district. Most of this ministry was among the tribal people. Many people came to the Lord through signs and wonders. There was a group of displaced people from Kandamal[46] among whom the CEA started a ministry. Several of these displaced persons were rehabilitated and a church was established among them. In addition, a few graduates of NTC and from local training centers, moved to Kalahandi district and started a ministry. In these two districts the primary focus is on people groups like the Oram, Turi, Dambo, Luhura, Munda, and Khadia.

Pastor Lamuel Pattnaik focused his ministry in Sambalpur district. He ministered mainly among the urban middle class in Sambalpur town and extended the work among the tribal groups in the outskirts and the villages. There were a number of stagnant and backslidden Christians because of the ineffectiveness of the mainline churches in ministering to them. When Pastor Lamuel started an effective work ministering to the needs of the people, many of them responded and joined his church as well as converts from Hinduism and tribal peoples. This work steadily grew and many churches were established. There was a revival in one tribal group called the Munda where several villages came to the Lord. Pastor S.K. Singh ventured into the Balangir district. He left his secular job after receiving a vision and conviction from God for ministry mainly among the Ganda and Mali people groups.

Orissa is the state in which the CEA has the most number of churches. The growth of the churches can be attributed to the response of certain people groups to the gospel, especially because of miracles, signs, and wonders. In the tribal and village areas there are mass movements. When a prominent person, like a village elder, comes to Christ, many times the whole village accepts Christ. The genuineness of their conversion experience can be questioned at times, but they are introduced to a new belief and the growth and transformation is slow but sure. The first generation Christians may find it difficult to detach themselves from their cultures and traditions, but the successive generations will definitely be different. The ministries of the CEA have grown stronger in the districts of Koraput, Sambalpur, Balangir, Sundargarh, Rayagada, and Kalahandi. In all, the CEA has around 100 churches in Orissa. Most are house churches, but there are a few church buildings too, as well as a primary school, a training center, and a children's home.

---

46   One of the biggest Christian persecutions broke out in Kandmal in 2008. Many Christians were killed, men were assaulted, women were raped and murdered, and several church buildings were vandalized.

In Orissa, the nature of the work was mainly gospel preaching and outreach ministry. Evangelists travelled from place to place, individually and in groups, with the gospel. In reaching a new place, evangelists contacted people and established a rapport with them and invited them to meetings, especially *bhajans*, a native way of presenting truth through songs with the help of local instruments. People are very interested in listening to *bhajans*, so they come together in groups and hear the gospel story and Biblical truths. Gospel films, like the Jesus film and *Dayasagar* ("Ocean of compassion" which is the story of Jesus) have helped a lot in attracting people and communicating the gospel. In villages, screening of a film is a rare event and it attracts many people. Dancing is also a way of life for the tribal people. Whenever they come together for some special occasion they get together to sing and dance. Skits, dramas, and tribal dancing were used to tell the gospel story to the people, and this has proved to be a very effective method. Such meetings were organized at special occasions like Easter and Christmas. Christmas is a very special time to invite thousands of people, as Indians, especially tribal peoples, have a special affection for celebrating festivals.

Another strategy used is to visit every house in a village and tell them about this new way of life, since other religious groups do not use this practice. It gives a special opportunity to listen to the problems and difficulties in the lives of people and to empathize with them and pray for them. Bible portions and gospel tracts are also given out. Once they realize that someone cares for them, they are open to come to meetings and listen to the gospel. People out of desperation come to the pastors and evangelists for prayer for deliverance from sicknesses and various types of bondage. Many miracles happen and people come to faith.

The church also uses philanthropic work to help the people in their distress. A group of displaced people was given housing and provisions, along with spiritual and emotional counseling, to help them settle in a new life. Another group of people were Christians, driven out of their homes by *jhasimulya*, a radical religious group. They were provided with tents and other supplies needed for them to settle down and start all over again. This strengthened their faith and confidence in Christ and as a result, they are strong followers of Jesus.

A couple of children's homes help the children of believers to have a better life and education, which also helps the character formation and spiritual growth of the children. In another area of Orissa, the church is opening primary schools to encourage the children of believers to study. In villages, children are encouraged to work in the fields or tend cattle rather than going to school. The church changed the whole attitude of parents and started sending children to school. This gave the pastors and teachers access to their homes and many people became open to the gospel and accepted Christ.

Miracles, signs, and wonders played a big role in bringing people to Christ. There are many stories of miraculous healing and deliverance from demon possession. One example is Kuntala, a childless Hindu woman who lived in Sambalpur district of Orissa, who followed all of the Hindu traditions and customs. She became very concerned and depressed, because being childless is considered a curse and people ridicule such women. Kuntala visited several temples and shrines, offered many *pujas* and sacrifices and spent much money to please the gods and goddesses, but she did not have a child in eight years of marriage. She visited hospitals and consulted doctors but nobody could help her, and her husband was contemplating divorce. One of her friends told her about a Christian church and a pastor and about the miracles that happened to people who went there for prayer. Kuntala went to the pastor, and shared her predicament and frustration with the pastor. He shared the gospel and the stories of Hannah and Elizabeth with her and told her of the power of Jesus Christ to do miracles. Then he anointed her with oil and prayed for her and asked her to continue to pray in the name of Jesus. A year later she came to the church with a baby girl and gave her testimony. She and her whole family put their trust in Christ and became believers of the church. Now she has three children. When a miracle happens in a place in the name of Jesus, many people put their trust in Christ, because Christ has done what millions of gods and goddesses could not do for them.

Arunachal Pradesh/Assam

The CEA ministry began among a small group of South Indian Malayalees who were working in Arunachal Pradesh. They initially started a prayer meeting at their houses and later started a Sunday worship service. Brother T. V. Mathai and Brother T. V. Thomas were the key people in these initial meetings. Pastor K. P. Philipose later joined this group after six months of theological education at New Theological College and he took the pastoral role. This group attracted mainly local people such as Nishis, Apatanis, Adis and others who worship the Sun and the Moon gods, Donyi-Polo and Abo-Tani, the original ancestors for most of these tribes.

Initially, the ministry in Arunachal and Assam was spread through word of mouth. The ones who were in faith shared their experience and faith to their friends and colleagues and they in turn shared with others. Apart from this, the main tool of spreading the Gospel was through spiritual meetings held in different places at different points of time. This was supported by regular prayer and fasting. In all these areas, we can find that the human effort was supported by the work of the Holy Spirit in convincing people of the Gospel message as well as through miracles. Believers were filled with the anointing of the Holy Spirit and started speaking in tongues, which is a peculiarity of the CEA in Arunachal and Assam. The church also ventured into ministering to the needs of the people by establishing a couple of children's homes and a school. Currently, there are about 40 churches in Arunachal and Assam.

As Hinduism does not have a strong hold in this region of India, there was a spiritual vacuum and when the gospel reached them, they responded very quickly. In addition, the power and work of the Holy Spirit was powerfully manifested in Arunachal and Assam. People were anointed with the gifts of speaking in tongues and prophecy. Miracles happened quite often. Unlike other places, in Arunachal the people who responded to the gospel were not from the lower strata. Many of them are from the higher sections of society, especially high officials in the government and skilled people like doctors, engineers and lawyers. This gave the church an extraordinary level of acceptance among other people in the community.

The Gospel has penetrated into the hearts of believers. Earlier, every individual was influenced by their traditional customs of polygamy and alcohol addiction. Polygamy was accepted in most of Arunachal Pradesh as a greater number of wives gives more status to a man in the society. Polygamy was discouraged inside the Church, and those who were unmarried were taught to have only one wife. Those who already had multiple wives were asked to maintain them and not to divorce as this would lead to other social issues. Another custom of Arunachal Pradesh is taking the elder brother's wife as a wife if one's elder brother dies. This still continues and the church is looking for a solution to this. Another major problem was *opo* or "rice-beer" addiction. Traditionally, men and women used to make rice beer at home and use it, which led to poverty, ill-health, and family disputes. Believers left this habit and were blessed with good-health, increased savings, and increased peace within their houses.

Arunachal Pradesh is traditionally animistic and has traditional festivals like Nyakum, Myoko, etc., in which animals are sacrificed. This tradition still continues; however, believers stay away from these rituals of spirit-worship. Usually, the people of Arunachal Pradesh carry a *dao*, or knife, all of the time. The Christian faith has given them an assurance of protection by Christ so they have stopped carrying knives. Traditionally, the people of Arunachal Pradesh did not have a concept of forgiveness, but believed in an eye for an eye, a life for a life. The virtue of forgiveness was introduced into Arunachal Pradesh by the Gospel, and as a result much social turmoil has been solved.

The growth of the church in Arunachal Pradesh has taught many similar lessons as in the other regions. The easiest way of penetrating into a new community with the Gospel is through word of mouth to close friends and relatives. This was the first step of the movement in Arunachal Pradesh. The initial sharing by word of mouth must be accompanied by regular spiritual meetings and fasting. Later, the spiritual meetings and fasting prayer at various different places led to the sudden growth of the Church. In all these attempts, the work of the Holy Spirit through the conviction of the Gospel message and miracles played the most crucial part.

Practices

The CEA's first priority is preaching the Gospel and planting churches. At the same time we recognize that God deeply cares for the whole person. As millions in India are trapped in the vicious cycle of poverty, we cannot close our eyes to basic human needs and just preach the Gospel. (See above the discussion on James 2:15-16). Therefore the goal of Christian Evangelistic Assemblies is to bring holistic transformation to individuals and communities.

In obedience to the Great Commission to make disciples of all nations (*ethne*), the CEA's primary goal is to preach the gospel and plant churches in places where the gospel has not been preached yet. We are convinced that this can be achieved more effectively by native evangelists, so potential leaders with conviction and commitment to win their own people for Christ are identified and trained for one year on the basic doctrines of the Bible and on principles and methods of mission and evangelism. These people have been sent to their own villages and people, where they are well accepted. As they are "sons of the soil" they are able to communicate the Good News in their own language and culture a lot more efficiently than an "outsider."

In most cases, one or two house churches are formed within several months. In some cases strong congregations take shape in a year or two. Team leaders keep in constant touch with the new workers by visiting them regularly. The new workers are gathered together on a regular basis for ongoing training and encouragement. Once a house church or congregation has at least seven baptized members, the CEA recognizes that worshipping group as a church.

Signs and miracles play a prominent role in attracting people to Jesus Christ and the church. The rural communities are poor, deprived of medical facilities, and suffer from all kinds of minor and major ailments. The people are also very superstitious and possessed by demons and evil forces. When affected, their only way out is to approach a shaman and obey what he commands. Often this will result in a financial loss, continued sickness, and even the loss of life. Many times, as a last resort, people will come to the church for prayer. Often God's power is manifested powerfully and people are healed of sickness and delivered from demon possession. This has a great impact on the minds of people and helps them to believe in a God who could do greater things than their traditional gods and goddesses. Not only the person who experienced deliverance, but his/her family, and sometimes the whole community also believes in Jesus Christ and becomes Christian.

A case in point occurred in Kurumkel, a small village in Sundargarh district of Orissa at the Chhattisgarh border. Hanuman, the Hindu monkey deity, possessed one young girl of 18 years, from the neighboring village of Amalajore. When she was possessed she would climb trees and jump from one branch to another just like a monkey, often removing her clothes. Her parents took her to different witch doctors, offered many *pujas*, sacrificed chickens and goats to many deities, but nobody could help her. Then she was taken to various hospitals for treatment, but the doctors could not diagnose any particular disease and expressed their inability to help. The family became very frustrated and even contemplated killing their daughter because of the shame they had to face. One of the Christians in the neighboring village heard about the predicament of the family and visited them. He told them about his pastor and advised them to go to him to get prayer for the girl. When the pastor prayed for her she was possessed again and started manifesting. The pastor shared the gospel and asked them to participate in a fasting prayer for one week with him. The church and the family together fasted and prayed for one week and on the last day the girl started manifesting again and finally, after throwing her to the ground, the demon departed and she was completely delivered from the attack of the evil one. As a result, not only the whole family, but also most of the people in the village trusted in Jesus Christ and were baptized. The girl is now married and has two children, and there is a very strong church in Amalajore.

Church planting can also follow an Antiochian model where the mother church sends out missionaries to plant other churches in the nearby localities. The first step is to establish a "mother church." A new church is birthed when a committed person along with a few others start sharing the gospel and caring for the people in a particular area with the conviction to form a congregation. With the moral and financial support of a sending agency (in this case the CEA) this becomes easier. Following the Biblical principle of planting other churches (Acts 16:50), the "mother church" plants several branch churches. This is done through prayer cells, Bible studies where people are invited for fellowship and prayer. These groups slowly grow into small worshiping congregations. The "mother church" stands behind the church planter and supports him. The founding pastor passes on his vision, values, and beliefs to the church planter and a strong relationship between the two is maintained, although the branch church functions autonomously, it is under the supervision and guidance of the "mother church." The church reaches out to the local people through voluntary work to meet their needs such as literacy, feeding programs, skill training, etc. with potential possibilities of church planting. All of these projects are closely linked to one another and accountable to the "mother church."

Training church planters is crucial to this model. Graduates of the training center are equipped to face the challenges in ministry and are involved in pioneering churches. Many of them return to their own villages. It is also important to find out which is the best fitting church planting model in North India, ethnically, geographically, and culturally, in rural and urban settings. The challenge for church planters is to do a thorough investigation of the target people group to adopt a model befitting their worldview and culture. This may vary from caste to caste and people group to people group. Further, they need to know church models that will lead to a deeper understanding of how effectively people can be reached and churches planted.

Finding people to go into interior rural areas has posed a challenge. Bringing people from villages to formal Bible colleges, where better academics are required, is difficult, and many of the village folks would not be comfortable leaving their homes and families. The solution was to train them in their own places and environment. To face this challenge, the Christian Evangelistic Assemblies has started "Satellite Training Centers" in different parts of the country. The strategy is to identify committed believers who are motivated to share the gospel and bring them for one year intensive training in basic biblical doctrines and principles of mission and evangelism. After the completion of the course, they are sent back to their own people and villages. Many of them also work as tent makers, working as cattle herds and farmers and at the same time being involved in evangelism and preaching.

> We identify committed young men and women who are willing to undergo a training of one year and to work in their own villages. This has proved to be very effective. Presently CEA has seven such training centers. Eight to twelve people are selected and they are given systematic training in basic biblical doctrines, mission and evangelism and are sent to minister among their own people. Many of our churches are the result of the ministry of such evangelists.[47]

India has millions of orphans and abandoned children living in the streets. Many are sold into slavery and forced to work in very difficult and inhumane situations. Poor parents are unable to provide for their children. The CEA tries to help a few such children in its ministry areas, especially the children of believers. The CEA has four such children's homes (Assam, Arunachal, Bhopal, Sambalpur). These children are given good food, a better place to stay, a friendly atmosphere, good clothing, a good education, and above all, an upbringing in the fear of God. Had it not been for these children's homes, these children would never have received such an opportunity in their lives. The added advantage of these homes is that they build a rapport with the parents and other community members and open a bridge of communication. The pastors and the house parents have easy access to the homes of people and they are open to listen to the gospel. Besides, the seed of the Word that was sown in the hearts of the children will definitely bear fruit and hopefully they will grow as men and women of God.

The rural population is mostly illiterate and involved in farming and herding. They do not send their children to school, especially girls, but use them

---

47 Niyog 2011, pg. 32.

to help in domestic chores and in the fields. But, this is changing slowly and now people realize the importance of education to advance their lives. They want their children to get at least a primary education. In order to help them, the CEA has started four schools over the years. Besides education, the CEA uses schools as a means to instill morals and Christian values in young minds. Children are taught moral stories, Christian songs, and values that provoke them to search for the truth with the hope that one day the seeds would sprout, grow, and bring forth fruit. As in the case of the children's homes, the teachers in the schools, who are also evangelists, have greater acceptance and accessibility to the houses of the students and in the society. They take every opportunity to change the lives of the children for good, so they may become responsible citizens of the country and the Kingdom of God. A few pastors also help children in their learning process by providing tuition and help in doing their homework. This has proved to be an immense help for young children and motivated them to study harder.

From the ministry of the schools, it has been observed that several small Christian congregations have been established. The staff of the school is fully committed to reaching out to the community and to help them in whatever way possible. This has made significant changes in the lives of people – children have started receiving education, gained teaching in health and hygiene resulting in improved health, parents have become more aware of better living and financial management, and a ray of hope has shone in their minds for a decent and respectful life.

The CEA also has a few vocational training centers to train people, especially women, in skilled work with the aim to help them earn a living and support their family financially. There are five tailoring training centers run by the churches. Several young girls and women undergo training for six months in cutting and stitching. This enables them to acquire the basic skills to make clothes for their own use and for others. A few sewing machines are also provided for the very needy.

LEARNINGS

After 22 years the ministry, the Christian Evangelistic Assemblies have grown beyond expectations. Presently the ministry has spread to 14 states (Uttarakhand, Uttar Pradesh, Himachal Pradesh, Punjab, Haryana, Delhi, Madhya Pradesh, Chhattisgarh, Andhra Pradesh, Orissa, Jharkhand, Bihar, Assam,

Arunachal Pradesh) and the neighboring country of Nepal. The CEA has 450 worshipping congregations and around 417 pastors/evangelists. A good number of the churches are rural churches, however, the CEA has three major urban ministries – Saharanpur, Delhi, and Bhopal.

The CEA and its ministries can make a visible and lasting impact in the lives of people and in the communities where it works. Though we have worked hard in establishing churches and other supportive ministries, we have never attempted to make an evaluation of these ministries. It is time to make a study in order to assess the growth of the churches, the impact and the influence it has stamped on society, and the contributions it has made in the lives of people, families, and the society, as well as some of the failures that have occurred.

This case study of the Christian Evangelistic Assemblies' ministry reveals that the gospel has brought change and transformation to the lives of people and in the larger society. History also teaches that wherever the gospel has gone, the lives of people have been transformed. Generally, the changes that occurred were in the areas of a better lifestyle, even in behavior, speech, mannerism, and clothing, freedom from bad habits and addiction, better education for children, financial stability, integration of family, and above all creating a confidence in people that they can do better in life.

Social changes like breaking the walls of the caste system, a decline in polygamy and child marriage, unity among tribes, etc. cannot be ignored. All of these work together for the harmony and peace of the larger society. Spiritually, people learned to depend on God and pray in time of need and difficulties. There is also an aspiration to live a better and holy life, bring up children in discipline, and live in harmony with other people. In urban areas, one of the advantages is that people coexist without giving much importance to their caste and background, which is not very easy in a rural context. The city gives more job opportunities to people. In an urban situation, it will be easier for the church to reach out to people with the gospel. But the challenges are also great. The Christian Evangelistic Assemblies has played a pivotal role in taking the gospel to unreached people, in urban as well as rural settings. It has transformed the lives of people and brought changes in the social strata.

The ministries of the Christian Evangelistic Assemblies are founded on the mandate of Scripture found in Matthew 28:19-20, *"Therefore go and make disciples of all nations, baptizing them in the name of the Father and of the Son and of the Holy Spirit, and teaching them to obey everything I have commanded you."* One of the founding principles of the CEA is to take the gospel to all *ethna* (*jatis*, or people groups) to expedite the promise of the return of the Christ. *"And this gospel of the kingdom will be preached in the whole world as a testimony to all nations, and then the end will come"* (Matthew 24:14). India is a land that has 4693 people groups, out of which thousands are yet to be reached with the gospel. The CEA's effort is to reach the unreached in rural as well as urban contexts, and to train people and send them to minister among their own people, where they are well accepted and can communicate the gospel in their heart language.

Jesus said, *"I shall build my church and the gates of hades shall not overcome it"* (Matthew 16:18). One of the primary goals of Jesus was to establish the church. But as soon as the church was established, Satan and his kingdom started fighting to destroy it. The history of the church is replete with stories of the fight against the church and it still continues. The CEA also faces such challenges. There were direct attacks against our evangelists and pastors – many were beaten up and imprisoned, falsely accused and physically assaulted, church buildings were vandalized, pastors were threatened and intimidated, but in spite of all this, the church grew in number and stature. The gates of hell could not keep it down.

Following the ministry pattern of Jesus, our effort is to minister to the whole person – spiritual, physical, emotional, economic, social, educational. Though the main focus is renewal of heart and mind, it will not be effective without ministering to the other faculties. Jesus ministered holistically, he preached, taught, fed people, helped, healed, counseled, and did everything possible to win them. Our pastors and evangelists try to teach the importance of becoming new creation in every aspect. *"If anyone is in Christ, he is a new creation; the old has gone, the new has come"* (2 Corinthians 5:17). The story of Zacchaeus is a good example (Luke 19:1ff). The importance of leaving the old lifestyle, especially fighting against addiction to drugs and alcohol, using abusive language, abusing women and children, fornication and adultery, and adopting a godly way of life is stressed, but achieving it pragmatically is a distant dream. However, we have started witnessing the initial steps towards this goal. The transformation that we witness is based on Biblical principles. The Bible teaches about monogamy (1 Timothy 3:2, 3:12, Titus 1:6), forgiveness (Matthew 6:12, 6:15, 18:21), unity (Galatians 3:28), importance of family (1 Timothy 3:4-5, 5:4), importance of achieving knowledge and wisdom (James 1:5, Proverbs 1:7,

4:5). The CEA tries to attain this in the lives of their pastors and evangelists so that they can be examples and teach others.

One of the important reasons for the growth of the church is not just the preaching and hearing of the word of God, but also the miracles, signs, and wonders that happen. This brings an element of faith in a greater God who can do greater things than the gods and goddesses whom people have been serving for generations. This was one of the reasons for church growth in the first century also. In the book of Acts there are several examples. At the revivification of Tabitha many people put their trust in Jesus (Acts 9:36-43). In the same way, the extraordinary and miraculous healing by the touching of handkerchiefs and aprons by Paul (Acts 19:11-20) and the exorcism of the slave girl (Acts 16:16ff) prompted many people to trust in Jesus. It was not their knowledge of the scripture or their unwavering faith in God that prompted them to believe in Jesus, but it is the trust in a God who can do extraordinary and miraculous things. However, it is mandatory that they grow in the knowledge of scriptures, fellowship with God and others, and in holiness as expected by God. All through the ministry of the CEA there are scores, probably hundreds, of stories of miracles and exorcisms by which people are made whole physically and delivered. This attracts people to come, explore and, if possible, to experience it themselves. The church's responsibility is to minister to such people and the CEA tries to do exactly that.

The work of the Holy Spirit, especially speaking in tongues and prophecy, is also a means that helps the church to grow. We have experienced this especially in the region of Assam and Arunachal. Usually this is preceded by several days of fasting and prayer. When this happens, people experience a trance like feeling and experience unexplainable joy and peace in their lives. This encourages people to grow closer to God and receive boldness to witness about their experience to others.

FUTURE

The Christian Evangelistic Assemblies has ministered in the urban, semi-urban, and rural areas of 14 states of India for over two decades. During this process the CEA has gone through different experiences, encouraging as well as disappointing. This section is an attempt to explore the experiences the CEA has undergone as a Christian organization attempting church planting in a religious pluralistic country, and to make a few suggestions for the future of church revitalization in India based on these experiences.

Though the CEA has been in ministry for more than two decades, it has been unable to impart the vision of its founders to the bottom levels of the organization. Many ministers join for fellowship and some for financial benefits. Many of them do have a call and a burden for ministry, but their association to the organization may also be for personal gain. Very few of them see the ministry as their own, and many are concerned about their social status, income, and lifestyle, so commitment is lacking to some extent. In addition, the CEA was unable to build a strong rapport with churches and believers at the grassroots level. The relationship between the leadership and the pastors remained at a personal level and the pastors did not hand leadership down to the local believers. So, there is not a strong bond between the leadership and believers. Currently, efforts are being made to build up this rapport. One future long-term challenge is to train a more committed leadership to face future challenges.

The ministry of the CEA has mainly been limited to people of the lower and middle class, who seem to be responsive to the gospel. The higher class who actually controls the economic, religious, political, and administrative matters of the country mostly remains unreached. The reason, probably, is that they do not feel a need for God, as they seem to be self-sufficient and content. Besides, the fear of ostracism is a major factor that keeps people from responding to the gospel, which is a matter of great concern for the higher class. But in the case of the other groups, who face struggles and difficulties everyday, people turn to God for help and any ray of hope that comes into their lives is welcomed, and the gospel does that for them. But, if people of higher class could be reached, that would bring a totally different outlook among the rest of the people. Currently the CEA is unable to make a dent in that area and are praying and hoping for a solution. Another future long-term challenge is to find creative ways to minister to upper class Indians.

The CEA is mostly dependent on the help of churches and individuals from abroad, and already the government has many restrictions on bringing money into the country, especially for Christian ministries. As Indian churches are not financially self-sufficient, we are unable to make progress in church planting and related Christian ministries and hence lag behind, compared to our counterparts elsewhere. There will come a time when the Indian church will not be able to receive any funds from abroad, and the political and social scenarios are preparing for this. Foreseeing this trend, the CEA has tried to teach pastors and churches the importance of becoming financially self-sufficient. However, not much progress has been made in this area. Probably, one of the reasons for this problem is the financial difficulty that ministers experience. Most of the believers are first generation Christians and financially not sound. They are unable to take care of the needs of the pastor and the church, in addition, the teaching on Christian giving and tithing is not strong in the church, so people do not give and the church remains needy, while the pastor has to look for extra resources to survive. Unless the church learns to give, it will be difficult for the Indian church to survive. There are enough resources in India, however Christians are not taught to give sacrificially. In the Bible, 2 Corinthians says, "... *for in a severe test of affliction, their abundance of joy and their extreme poverty have overflowed in a wealth of liberality on their part. For they gave according to their means, as I can testify, and beyond their means, of their own free will, begging us earnestly for the favor of taking part in the relief of the saints ...*" 2 Corinthians 8:2-4 (RSV). This principle has to be practiced by Indian Christians and churches. A third future long-term challenge is to help the Indian church become completely self-sufficient at the local and national levels.

Most CEA congregations are house churches, which has both advantages and disadvantages. But in North India, where the caste system is very strong, people from different castes and people groups find it difficult to gather for worship in the house of a person from a different caste, especially if that person is from a lower caste, so people hesitate to come together to worship in house churches, though the situation has improved slightly. If worship is held in a common place, the problem is alleviated to a large extent. The Christian Evangelistic Assemblies wants to build as many church buildings as possible, but many things hinder this, such as the financial crisis, the inability to buy land in the name of the CEA due to land laws and regulations, and the opposition from fanatic religious groups. Such groups have destroyed some worship centers that have been built. Even in places where the situation is favorable to build, a lack of sufficient funds does not permit this. Another long-term future challenge is to develop creative, low cost ways for worship to break through caste barriers.

Another area, where the CEA has failed to make significant progress is the ministry among women. Women in Indian societies are hesitant to come to the forefront in any sphere, probably because they were suppressed for centuries and because of a lack of education. As Christ and the Bible have given equal status to women and men, the church has to make an effort to uplift and empower women. Half of the population is women, and without their active participation in Christian ministry, it will be impossible to reach other women, especially in rural areas. The CEA is training women (presently there are 16 women being trained) for reaching out to other women and it needs to see an aggressive effort in this area. The church also has a responsibility to find suitable matches for young girls and boys so that they can marry at the right age. This is one of the areas where we have failed. Many families do not want to come to church because of the uncertain future this situation raises in their minds and family discussions, especially among first generation Christians. A fifth future long-term challenge is to find ways to empower and strengthen Christian women and families within the Indian context.

The most important method to communicate a message to someone else is to tell it in his or her "heart language." This is one area where the Christian church lags behind. While there are Bibles and Christian literature in the major languages, there are hundreds of languages/dialects that do not have Bibles, Bible portions, or any other literature available. This handicaps our efforts to minister to people, as they do not have material they can read. Even in the major languages, though the Bible has been translated, the number of other Christian literature available is limited. Another future long-term challenge is to find lost cost effective ways to distribute Christian literature in multiple languages in rural as well as urban settings.

Indian societies are very complex. Their beliefs, customs, and traditions have been handed down through the generations and people are very proud of their legacy. A majority of people is unwilling to listen to and accept anything that is "foreign." So understanding the culture, language, worldviews, and mindset of people is very important in communicating the gospel to them. A particular method used for one people group may not, work for another group. So, the need today is to ascertain which model of church planting will best fit various cultural, geographic, and ethnic realities that exist in North India and select a model that best fits each people group. In addition, the focus of the church is to build the Kingdom of God and bring holistic transformation in the lives of people. This is not possible unless the church ministers to the needs of people, which was also the pattern of the ministry of Jesus Christ. Jesus healed, fed, taught, consoled, delivered, sympathized and empathized and above all gave them the hope of eternal life. The problem with many Indian churches is that only the need of salvation is emphasized and not much is done to make the lives of believers easy and comfortable. When a person is hungry and worried about his family, he will not be in a disposition to think of and meditate about transcendental things. The method of William Booth, i.e., soap, soup and salvation, seems to be the best model for Indian communities as many of them are downtrodden, harassed, needy, and poor. The CEA is trying to do this as much as possible within the limits of its resources, but more needs to be done. A seventh long-term future challenge is to develop culturally sensitive, holistic methods of church planting that can work effectively in the Indian context.

Miracles, signs, and wonders play a significant role in people coming to Christ. This may be incomprehensible for Western ideology, but it is a reality. Indian people are very religious and a good number are practicing their religion. There are a few who reason and try to find the truth, but even the highly educated people are often irrational when it comes to religion. Miracles, signs, and wonders prompt them to realize that there is a greater God and power that can go beyond what their gods and goddesses can do. This will always help people be open to Christianity, as many signs and miracles happen in the name of Jesus. One future long-term trend, which seems to remain central, is the need to focus on the power of the Holy Spirit to heal sickness, release people from bondage, and transform lives.

The Christian Evangelistic Assemblies has come a long way in the last two decades, but the road that stretches ahead is vast, considering the opportunities, challenges, and the need to reach 1.35 billion people with the gospel of Jesus Christ. We are barely scratching the surface and the task ahead is gigantic. Our hope and goal are to reach as many people as possible with the gospel and plant as many church as possible in the unreached places. Above all, our hope is to emerge as a holistic transformation agent shaping the minds and lives of people in all aspects, instilling Kingdom values, and thereby, rewriting the history of the Christian church in the land of India.

Works Cited

Board of Governors
    1992   *Minutes of the Board of Governors of the Christian Evangelistic Assemblies*, June 19, 1992.

    n.d.   *Memorandum of Association*, Christian Evangelistic Assemblies.

Joseph, P.V.
    2012   *A North Indian Mission Paradigm: Life and Vision of George Chavanikamannil, Beginnings*, Dehra Dun, India:NTC.

Reese, Robert
    2016   "Dependency: What is Dependency?" Blog from June 16, 2016. https://wmausa.org/our-mission/dependency/ (accessed 6/6/2017).

Samuel, Varghese
    2011   *Christian Evangelistic Assemblies: Celebrating God's Faithfulness for 20 years, Niyog 2011*, Dehra Dun, India: NTC.

    n.d.   Personal interview with Rev. Dr. George Chavanikamannil, Founder of Christian Evangelistic Assemblies.

Case Study Three: Allahabad Bible Seminary

J. Sundera Raj and Thomas M. J.

Abstract: Allahabad Bible Seminary, one of the leading seminaries in India, prepares young men and women for Christian Mission. It influences enormously the Christian Mission in India, especially, by preparing grass-root level missionaries to reach out in Indian villages with the transforming Gospel. Since its beginning, the seminary has not changed the motto and vision of the founding fathers who were led by the Holy Spirit. The Seminary gives special consideration to young men and women from remote areas of the Hindi speaking-belt. The seminary teaches in both Hindi and English. Many of the leaders of Christian mission organizations, churches, para-church organizations have received training from Allahabad Bible Seminary. For eight years, the Seminary has been witnessing the revitalization of the mission and vision for which it has been established.

DEFINITION

In 1939, Dr. Kilborne, an OMS Missionary in Japan, came to India to start a ministry in India. While he was travelling from Delhi to Kolkotta, at about midnight, someone woke him up and asked him to leave the train. He disembarked believing that it was the guidance of God. He got off with his luggage at Allahabad Junction. In the morning, he prayerfully walked around the city, and he came to the area of the civil hospital (Baily Hospital). He was led to a compound opposite from the hospital that was used as a hostel for the nurses of the hospital. He enquired about the compound and prayed about it. After going back to the United States, he sent a team of 7 missionaries and started a center in 1941. They purchased the same land which he prayed over and started the Seminary.

Allahabad Bible Seminary (ABS) was established in July 1942 under the auspices of One Mission Society, formerly known as the Oriental Missionary Society and OMS International respectively, which aims to see the Gospel of Jesus Christ spread throughout the world and to see God glorified in all that we say and do. The Seminary was launched with 18 students at a revival and holiness convention. In the initial stage, the OMS staff was headed by Dr. Eugene and Mrs. Esther Erny (former OMS missionaries to China), who were joined by Wesley and Betsy Duewel, new recruits from the United States. Charles A. Cowman, founder of the Society in Japan in 1901, believed strongly in the importance of well-trained nationals for the growth and development of the Church, and they were guided by the ministry philosophy of OMS (viz. A trained corps of national workers focused on evangelism with the goal of planting indigenous Churches). The format of ABS training is centered on biblical studies, development of spiritual life, and practical experience in evangelistic outreach.

It was begun with the sole purpose of training native pastors, evangelists and church planters. It focuses on effective preparation for Spirit-filled ministry with a deeper concern for winning men and women to Christ in India. It is an evangelical theological institution with an ecumenical outlook that trains committed men and women for effective fruitful ministry in India and abroad. Major denominational churches, para-church organizations, and missionary societies send their candidates to the Seminary for theological education. We provide theological education within the evangelical framework with a societal commitment. We cater a relevant theological orientation for the students to respond to the needs and challenges of the Church and Society in the 21st century. Our ministerial and academic programs are structured with the sole purpose of communicating the life transforming and liberative message of the Gospel to transform society.

The Seminary is located at 60/64, Stanley Road, Allahabad, Uttar Pradesh just opposite the Civil Hospital, on a spacious nine-acre campus, which provides a setting for quiet study and devotion. Allahabad, with a population of about two million people is located in the densely populated Ganges valley, where there exists great scope for sharing Christ in hundreds of villages, which are almost entirely without a Christian witness. At the junction of the Ganges and Jamuna Rivers (the "Sangam"), Allahabad is a holy place for Hindus, visited annually by millions of pilgrims. The nearby Allahabad University and numerous colleges provide the intellectual stimulation of an educational center. Thus situated in a multi-religious-cultural center, ABS students are able to learn the best cross-cultural approaches to a wide range of people such as *mela* crowds, university students, villagers, and urban residents who represent all the major religions of India.

Since its inception, Allahabad Bible Seminary has produced many church leaders, seminary teachers, theologians, social workers, evangelists, church-planters etc… for the Indian Church. Our graduates have been doing commendable work in their respective ministerial locations. This is evident from the appreciatory comments of the church leaders of different faith traditions. The Seminary faculty and students also have opportunities to hear many Christian leaders and speakers, both Indian and foreign, who visit the churches and institutions of the city. As opportunity affords, such visitors are also invited to speak in the Seminary chapel services.

CONTEXT

The Mission Statement for ABS reads:

Founded by OMS International, Allahabad Bible Seminary exists primarily to serve the Evangelical Church of India as well as the whole Church of Christ, particularly in North India.

Allahabad Bible Seminary aims to train and equip young men and women for pioneer evangelism and church planting by providing sound evangelical theological education and in-depth pastoral formation. It is a denominational Seminary of the Evangelical Church of India with a nation wide interdenominational vision and outreach.

The basic purpose of Allahabad Bible Seminary is the effective preparation of Spirit-filled ministers with a deeper concern for winning men and women to Christ and for building up His body in India.

The Seminary aims to maintain a Bible-centered teaching format with a contemporary emphasis. This is done in a setting that is thoroughly evangelical in theology, and with a strong practical emphasis on holiness of thought and life. The Bible is recognized as the supreme authority in all matters of faith and practice and is interpreted in harmony with the historic evangelical understanding of the Christian faith.

The seminary seeks to maintain high educational standards and follow sound teaching methods to integrate supervised fieldwork with other aspects of the curriculum. An attempt is made to relate each subject so far as possible to the needs of the Church in India.

The seminary emphasizes evangelism, church planting, and practical ministerial activities. It Statement of Faith reads as follows:

We believe that the Bible is the inspired, the only infallible, authoritative Word of God.

We believe that there is one God, eternally existent in three Persons, Father, Son and Holy Spirit.

We believe in the deity of our Lord Jesus Christ in His virgin birth, in His sinless life, in His miracles, in His atoning death through His shed blood, in His bodily resurrection, in His ascension to the right hand of the Father, and in His pre-millennial return in power and glory.

We believe that for the salvation of lost and sinful humanity, regeneration by the Holy Spirit is absolutely necessary.

We believe in the present ministry of the Holy Spirit by whom the believer is sanctified and enabled to live a holy life.

We believe in the resurrection of both the saved and the lost: they that are saved to the resurrection of life, and they that are lost unto the resurrection of damnation.

We believe in the spiritual unity of believers in our Lord Jesus Christ.

DEVELOPMENT

The Allahabad Bible Seminary is one of the few theological seminaries in India that offers courses in both English and Hindi. This is to train people to meet the needs of the churches especially in North India. The Seminary has an experienced faculty and a well-equipped computerized library.

Allahabad Bible Seminary offers a Bachelor of Divinity (B.D.) program, the basic theological program of the Senate of Serampore College (University). It is offered in two categories: a Bachelor of Divinity completed in five years, in both English and Hindi for 12th pass candidates, and a Bachelor of Divinity completed in four years, in both English and Hindi for graduates of any discipline from a recognized university.

In addition, ABS offers theological education by extension in both Hindi and English, which aims to educate lay people theologically to do ministry and to mold the faith community in its respective contexts. ABS provides specially prepared course material and facilitates the students in meeting their teachers and tutors for discussion and exposure to Christian ideals. At present, we offer three streams of theological education by extension: a Bachelor of Theological Studies (B.T.S.) in four years for 12th pass or fail candidates, a Bachelor of Christian Studies (B.C.S.) in four years for graduates of any discipline from a recognized university, or a B.Th. with Second Class.

Currently the student body consists of 173 residential students, representing 23 states and 38 language groups, with 121 studying in English and 52 studying in Hindi. The Seminary has achieved a passing rate of 98% in the semester examinations. In addition, there are 1,210 extension students, with 1,088 studying for the Bachelor of Theological Studies, 110 for the Bachelor of Christian Studies, and 12 for the Diploma in Christian Studies.

Practices

The practical work department of Allahabad Bible Seminary plays an important role in undertaking the objectives of ABS through its activities. Allahabad Bible Seminary tries to keep academic as well as practical work in balance. Under the proficient leadership of the principal, with the advice of the faculty members and with the enthusiastic participation of all the students at ABS, the practical works department is working toward greater transformation in and around Allahabad city and the district through various kinds of ministries.

Children and Youth Ministries

Children and youth have a very important place in the practical ministry of Allahabad Bible Seminary. We participate in children's ministry in the villages, through which we are able to contact parents and form closer relationships with the adult members of the villages. We also help the churches in their existing Sunday schools. In addition, our students go to three different schools in the city and raise awareness about various social evils in the society through songs and stories during the morning assembly. We also try to spread the gospel in various available mediums. As a result we have adopted the method of using puppets in our ministry, and we have found that it is an effective method to reach out to the villagers and their children.

Ecclesiastes 12:1 says, "Remember your creator in the days of your youth." Youth is the time where one decides many things about the direction of his/her life. Often we find youngsters are caught up in various kinds of bad habits and become addicts of drugs, alcohol, and other harmful behaviors, so we try to help them find the right path and decide what is best for their life. To encourage them, ABS organizes youth programs, in which they are allowed to explore their talents through music, singing, and other avenues. Seminars are arranged through SCMI to make them aware of various social evils corrupting our society, and try to equip them to face challenges in their lives. We are also involved in the youth programs of various local churches of different denominations, and help the youngsters make positive decisions. In addition, we help churches conduct youth fellowships and other youth programs.

Literacy Projects

When we visit many villages with the gospel, we find that the villagers are not in a position to read and write because of low levels of literacy. For various reasons, there are lots of school dropouts in these families, so we meet the parents and explain to them the importance of education and appeal to them to give their children more education. While visiting the villages, we also help the children who do attend school with their school lessons.

In many of the villages, the adults are uneducated and do not know the importance of education. Hence, along with raising awareness about literacy, we are helping them to read and write. In order to help the adult members of many villages in a systematic way, we are planning to start adult literacy programs in a few villages soon. This will help them improve their living standards and enable them to know what is happening in the world. This also would help them in their trade and daily transactions, while developing a better life style.

Health Outreach

The Seminary students and faculty also visit sick people in the hospitals, share our empathy with them and pray for them. If they are willing, we leave tracts and gospel booklets for them to read. In the future, we are planning to extend this ministry to more hospitals in Allahabad.

Another health related outreach is an outreach ministry team that is working in a village called Logharah about 45 kilometers away from ABS. Most of the people living in this village are snake charmers. The living conditions in this village are very poor. There are no hygienic facilities in the village and good drinking water is not available. Since there is not a proper water source in this village, the people are not able to bathe regularly, and do not trim their nails or hair. Through the practical ministry team, we teach them good habits and raise their awareness about cleanliness and hygiene. We also cut children's nails and teach them to be neat and clean. In addition, there is little awareness about family planning. Even ladies of 55 years of age have small children. Khelwa is another village where a woman of 35 years of age has 8 children. In order to help them, sometimes we take medical personalities to explain to them about family planning. We are also planning to conduct regular medical camps in a few of these villages, where they do not have any medical facilities or proper transportation system. We believe this effort will help the villagers in a minimal way to improve their health conditions and thus benefit their lives.

Social Outreach

Allahabad Bible Seminary believes in a holistic ministry, which involves helping the poor and needy through the generous giving of the faculty and students. Often we visit orphan children in Mother Teresa's Missionaries of Charity homes, spend time with them, and help the children with some gifts. In the winter, we find that there are lots of poor people and rickshaw drivers sleeping on the footpaths and in railway stations without proper clothes to protect them from the cold. One humanitarian way we help is to collect blankets and winter clothes from faculty and students to give them. This is another small way we try to identify ourselves with the everyday struggles of the poor sections of our society.

The Leprosy Mission (TLM) is doing a tremendous job in various ways, especially in the midst of people affected with leprosy. It is well known that lepers are living with a great social stigma. We visit the TLM hospital in Naini very often and spend time with the patients. It's amazing to talk with them and to get to know about their feelings and emotions. We also share our love with them through sharing food and other resources. TLM Naini has a chapel where a worship service is conducted for the patients, staff, and for nearby villagers. ABS faculty members also help them in their spiritual activities by worshiping with them every Sunday and sharing God's word with them. It is a great blessing to them as well as ABS.

In the early church, believers gathered in houses for prayer and fellowship. ABS follows these Biblical principles and has started worship groups in different places in and around Allahabad. At present we have seven such groups. People gather there every Sunday with faith and enthusiasm, where singing, witnessing, praying, sharing of the word of God, and fellowshipping are the main features. Our students and faculty members are involved in this ministry with great joy, and we are planning to start such worship groups in other places as well.

Women's Ministries

The women's ministry of Allahabad Bible Seminary is one of the main sources of ministerial exposure for the female students. Generally, women's ministry comes under the practical ministry department of ABS. God has enabled us to start this ministry among the women in different villages in the Allahabad district. Through this ministry, we proclaim the good news among the women in different villages and raise awareness of spiritual, social and physical evil, and types of bondage. The female students of ABS and the women faculty members are actively involved in this ministry.

The women's ministry faces many challenges. Almost all of the women in the villages where we concentrate are illiterate, daily laborers (such as domestic servants, stone breakers, farm laborers, etc.). There is not much teaching on morality, and as a result the future of many girls in the villages is at risk. There are often very poor understandings of health and hygiene, and a lack of knowledge about health care. The economic situation is very precarious with unemployment and financial crisis as a constant threat, so they are not able to afford basic necessities or education for their children. As a result, the majority of the children do not go to school, and even if they go, most dropout from school after the 5th or 6th grade.

Future aims plan to establish a free medical camp (to teach on health and hygiene), an adult education program to train the women to read and write, help for the children's education (including free tuition and financial help for the children), the implementation of a self-employment program, social and moral teaching (on issues such as finances, family planning, marriage, and addictions), and a counseling program. We also hope to conduct a women's retreat, where we bring the women from all these villages onto our Seminary campus and have a one-day retreat where we can teach them on different topics to improve their lives and encourage them to leave behind the social stigmas that bind them. In the process, we will encourage them by having fellowship and receiving love with other people as they grow in their knowledge of Jesus Christ.

A women's fellowship was also started at ABS to give some spiritual nourishment and training to the wives of the married students. Today, it is part of the spiritual formation curriculum. Women faculty members, married ladies, and all of the female students meet once a week on Wednesday afternoons for Bible study, worship, prayer, and fellowship. ABS Women's Fellowship emphasizes the spiritual and Christian responsibilities of women in church and family. It wants to impart knowledge and awareness, as well as develop personal skills. Everyone, especially the graduating women students have been involved actively as a learning experience for future ministry among women. Alternately the graduating women and the involved women faculty members take turns preparing the Bible studies. The topics are selected in such a way that they emphasize issues relevant for women.

Ministry to the Street Children

ABS is involved in caring for street children. The very mention of the word 'street children' leaves us thinking about scenes of infants lying naked on heaps of tones as their mothers toil away breaking stones or doing other work on the roadside, children looking for fragments of food from garbage dumps, children huddling up at night on the pavement, under a bridge, in drain pipes or in some unclaimed shelter, trying to cover themselves with a piece of dirty cloth during chilly nights, children in tattered clothes, who have possibly never washed, playing, gambling, or engaged in various covert or overt forms of begging, etc., Whatever may be the activity pursued by the street children they have a few things in common: lack of parental care, love, protection and supervision, and lack of general education and chances for adequate mental development.

Street children among whom ABS is involved can be categorized as:

1. Children on the Street: this category consists of children working on the streets but who maintain more or less regular ties with their families.

2. Children of the Street: Children in this category maintain only tenuous relations with their families, visiting them only occasionally.

3. Abandoned Children: this category completely cut off all ties with their biological families and are completely on their own.

Our team is involved with education among the first category. In the evening, most days about five o'clock, team members give basic education to children on the street. However at times we are not able to advance this education since the children's families constantly move from one place another.

Second and third category childern are the difficult groups. Most of them use drugs and are involved with various criminal activities. Among these childern our students build rapport and develop networks. They share their problems with the team. Team members give counseling, and extend care, protection and love. We can see their love and affinity towards us. We regularly visit railway stations and spent time with them.

Religious Ministry for Students and Faculty

Sermon evaluation is one important feature of Allahabad Bible Seminary. It is used to teach the students to preach the Word of God systematically and meaningfully. Usually sermon evaluation is conducted on Thursdays between 2:30 PM to 4:00 PM, when the faculty and students will be assigned to evaluate the sermons of students preached in the chapel. In the sermon evaluation students are taught and reminded of the need for contextualizing their sermons.

The Ministry Fellowship Groups meet every Wednesday between 9:45AM to 10:20AM. Each fellowship group consists of one or two faculty members and 8-10 students. The concerned group meets regularly to share personal or community concerns and to uphold the Seminary family and the group members in prayer. In this fellowship, the faculty and students spend time for prayer, devotion, and fellowship. The purpose of this fellowship group is to bring the Seminary family more closely together and to make the community life vibrant.

Once in a month, we as a family conduct a Community Communion Service between 5:30 PM to 7:00 PM. The aim of this service is to allow the entire Seminary family to partake in Holy Communion together. Faculty and students conduct and celebrate the Communion, which provides not only spiritual nourishment, but also ministerial exposure to the student community.

Regional fellowships make Allahabad Bible Seminary a multi-lingual and multi-cultural Christian Worship Center. The Allahabad Mizo Christian Fellowship is held on every Sunday afternoon between 3:00 PM – 4:30 PM. The South Indian Fellowship meets every Saturday at 7:45 PM. The Tamil – Malayalam Fellowship is held every Sunday from 5:00 PM onwards. The North East Fellowship convenes its worship every Sunday at 5:00 PM. The Hindi Aradhana Sangati conducts its worship fellowship at 5:30 PM every Saturday and the Presbyterian Fellowship has been held weekly on Saturday between 5:00 PM – 6:30 PM.

The Annual Spiritual Life Convention is another venture of Allahabad Bible Seminary. It is conducted in the month of February, and gives an opportunity to the Seminary family and the Christian communities in Allahabad to hear soul stirring messages from well-known preachers.

The Student Missionary Fellowship is another salient feature of Allahabad Bible Seminary. It aims to raise mission awareness among the members of the Seminary family. Our students visit churches in and around Allahabad to encourage other believers to engage and support the mission activities of the Seminary. The SMF conducts an annual missionary conference and raises funds for the mission activities of Seminary.

Student Christian Movement-India (SCMI)- the Allahabad Bible Seminary Unit is an integral part of SCMI, and it is functioning as the local facilitator to implement various programs. SCMI and ABS agree on the issues and principles of the Christian faith and the burden to share the Gospel, so the relationship between SCMI through the ABS-Unit has been to smoothly work together helping to carry out the task of ministry. The ABS-Unit is a long-standing partner to SCMI and vice versa where the cause of the Gospel comes first. The ABS-Unit functions under a governing body which is formed under the inspiring leadership of the ABS principal from the present student body. It is a well-represented diverse body, and it lasts for a year.

The ABS-Unit facilitates various academic and community development programs, while the office bearers implement the ethos of SCMI, and so are involved in uplifting needy students and creating awareness on various socio-religious issues to equip students to face the challenges of the church and society in a more effective way. In the academic year for 2009-2010 we have started programs such as an English Language Course and a Basic Computer Course. These programs are mainly for the students from poor backgrounds. We conduct classes three times a week (Monday, Wednesday, and Friday).

Music has always played an important part in the cultural and devotional life of the Seminary. Each year Hindi and English choirs are organized, and they perform in Seminary programs as well as in other churches and functions in Allahabad.

Along with spiritual and academic activities, ABS is involved with sports activities under the leadership of the Committee of Sports and Games, headed by the Director of Sports and Games. The Director is a faculty member chosen annually by the principal. Similarly, one sports captain and two vice-captains are also chosen by the student body to represent men and women. The Seminary's sports program includes weekly compulsory game periods. These consist of volleyball, badminton, football, cricket, and various indoor games such as table tennis, chess and carrom. Students are allowed to engage in sports activities between 4:00PM and 6:00PM. Annual Sports Day is the culmination of all sports activities for which the Seminary community is prepared. Besides this, there could be either a soccer or cricket match between staff and students. The ABS Team also participates in Inter-Church Cricket Tournaments in Allahabad City.

The Social and Religious and Cultural (SARAC) Committee is one of the important organs of Allahabad Bible Seminary. It takes care of all the activities and functions related to the social, religious, and cultural aspects of the Seminary family (*Freshers' Welcome Nite, Independence Day Flag Hoisting, Christmas Bonfire, Day of Labour (*Sram Dan*), Christmas Caroling, Republic Day Flag Hoisting Ceremony, Extempore Speech Competition, Farewell Function, Cultural Show* etc.) The Committee is comprised of two faculty in-charge and the class representatives. Cultural Programs are organized from time to time especially on Independence Day, Republic Day etc. During Christmas celebrations the Seminary community also performs carol singing by different linguistic and cultural groups. The cultural programs help the Seminary family taste the beauty of Indian cultural diversity.

Academic Outreach

Allahabad Bible Seminary entered into the arena of publishing theological books, journals, etc. to encourage creative theological discourse and to nourish the spiritual life of the faith community in India. *ABS Journal*, the theological journal of Allahabad Bible Seminary, is published three times a year to encourage relevant theological narratives to enrich the theological community. *Aletheia*, an annual magazine of the Seminary is also published to bring out the literary creativity of the students and faculty of the Seminary.

The Centre for the Study of Indian Culture and Society (CSICS) has also been created as a way to further academic understanding of India and its culture. Various programme of the Centre are as follow:

- The Centre conducts a Refresher Course for village evangelists and missionaries.

- The Centre launches its journal, named the *Journal of Mission and Intercultural Studies*, which offers a forum for the study of the various facets of Mission and Intercultural Studies in the Indian Subcontinent. The journal facilitates a discussion forum for scholars in theological and mission academia especially in the areas of mission, religion, and cultural studies. As the name suggests, the journal shall explore the areas covered by mission and cultural studies in the Indian context. It attempts to provide knowledge and understanding of the theological, historical, cultural, and sociological aspects involved in doing Christian mission in Asia especially in India.

- The Centre is aimed to launch grass-root level research focusing on various communities, their cultures, indigenous movements, etc., and also started to work on the Resource Centre for Mission and the Study of Indian Religions. Various books, dictionaries and encyclopedias that deal with Indian religion, culture and society have been purchased and a resource centre in the form of a library has been set up. The primary goal of this library is to equip Christian workers with an informed knowledge of Indian religion and culture.

LEARNINGS

When God designs a plan, God brings together people of different cultures, languages, races, and traditions, who come from various socio-economic and political backgrounds. The ministry of Allahabad Bible Seminary is an example of God's plan and vision that is designed for the people of India, especially North India.

The vision that was given to ABS founding fathers was transferred to the next generation of overseas missionaries, and was then transferred to Indian leadership, and it still continues to be transfered. Thus, ABS leads by vision. ABS focuses mainly on church planting ministry, for which many young men and women have been receiving training for seventy-one years.

However, the vision of ABS was more shaped and enlarged mainly due to the revitalizing process, which began eight years before. There are various factors that contributed in revitalizing the mission and vision of Allahabad Bible Seminary. Those aspects are as follows:

(i) To heal the community, leadership took the initiative to begin family meetings in the faculty-staff quarters. It is to heal the scars in the lives of the people living within the community.

(ii) Initiative in the healing process led to the movement of the people (community) into various mission fields. Leadership moved at first into the field which triggered interest among others. It was a move of faith, which God honored and provided everything needed.

(iii) A process of pruning was necessary which was facilitated by the smooth departure of some who disagreed with the new process.

(iv) Breaking the hierarchy was done with:

(a) A personal touch.
(b) Accessibility to the principal.
(c) Direct confrontation-correction at a personal level.

(v) The principal functioned by imitating a model received from missionaries:

(a) Morality and integrity
(b) Simplicity and humility
(c) Service not power

(vi) Steps were taken to deal with the obstacles created by the involvement of foreign missionaries. It was decided not to build church buildings under the ABS banner. The churches must take the responsibility to build it.

(vii) Self-reliance of the seminary is a goal for 2017 which curtails external involvement into our day-to-day works.

Keys factors that contributed to revitalization:

(i) Prayer

(ii) Focusing on vision and mission

(iii) Creating a community with integrity

(iv) Wise counselors

(v) Family support

Areas of revitalization in mission:

The following areas in the mission revitalization have been seen for the past few years.

They are as follows:

(i) Inherited mission from Ishu Darbar (preachers and healers): areas of mission were then located with a slogan "*Ishu darbar, aapke dwar par*" (Jesus is at your door) and ministry was continued.

(ii) Openness fostered among the village women. It results in their relationship with people including interaction with men on the basis of equality, health and hygiene issues are discussed, legal information as part of their empowerment is undertaken, teachings about HIV with the help of NGO/experts, women literacy programs etc.,

(iii) Seminary has teaching courses which equip students to understand a fuller picture of the reality in the mission fields. This helps in recognizing the socio-cultural and religious-political issues present in the field and take up a focused mission. For example, a street children ministry was undertaken by the college where students get exposure to understand the various challenges of the people and see their lives in relation to their theoretical knowledge as well as their call and commitment. It helps in training to relate ministers to specific contexts. Areas of students' lives are challenged and they undergo socio-cultural changes in their personal lives as well.

(iv) Through the revitalization of mission, visible factors of socio-spiritual changes in the lives of the people are as follows:

- Children's education is supported with free tuition with a visible outcome since these children are doing well in their studies,
- Creating awareness about issues like violence within families has brought a positive effect upon the larger family unit,
- Health and hygiene issues are addressed by regularly teaching children by cutting hair, nail cutting, wearing clean clothes, giving daily bath, etc. Though it is a slow process, changes are visible in their lives,
- Adult literacy program has started helping people to read and write,
- Centre for the Study of Indian Culture and Society, as a resource center, brings in people for fifteen days in order to equip them in understanding and analyzing their own culture to enable them to do more effective mission, understanding the contextual realities. The outcome of

this course is evident by looking at the worldview changes in the lives of the missionaries,

- ABS ministry creates hope for the people as a revitalizing mission. It is mainly through producing spiritual fruit through the life of the community and exercising the spiritual gifts. For example, in many places it is evident, healing as a result of prayer gives people hope for a brighter future. A paradigm shift is visible in the life of the villagers (women, children, and men) which includes economic, social, and other areas.

Divine action can most readily be seen in the revitalization process:

There are many times divine intervention can be seen as evidence in the life of the people as well as ABS community. A few examples are:

(i) Signs and miracles: For example a childless couple bearing a child after our prayer where the villages recognized it as God's activity.

(ii) Change in students' worldview: Often this is due to going to villages and experiencing a shift in their understanding during their life in ABS.

(iii) Villages turning strong in faith and becoming motivators to others to withstand opposition and persecution at the local level. The footprint of the Holy Spirit is also seen in the testimonies of the people.

(iv) Shift in campus life in ABS: For example, a missional focus in everything they undertake.

Revitalization of ABS mission and theological/biblical concepts, stories, or meanings:

Revitalization of the mission of ABS is closely related to following biblical concepts as well as stories:

(i) In the story of Philip being led by the Holy Spirit in the Acts of the Apostles we find correlations with the ABS mission. It helps in having a Spirit-led ministry.

(ii) Preaching to everyone (Acts 1:8).

(iii) Teaching and discipline everyone (Matt. 29:18-20).

(iv) The biblical theme of equality and brotherhood in Christ is taught.

(v) ABS' mission success is inherited from the labor of others done earlier (1 Cor. 1).

Key persons, church, or other experiences related to mission:

The revitalization of Allahabad Bible Seminary's mission, though it is a team effort, has many individual contributions that should be noted, those key persons are:

(i) Rev. Paul Sigamony, Dean of Practical Work, has had a major role in the mission of ABS. Eight years ago; he took charge of practical work. Before joining ABS, he had rich experience in a church planting ministry. He could relate his vast experience to the vision and mission of ABS. He, therefore, contributes in revitalizing the vision of ABS.

(ii) The Extension Department of ABS, through its various extension which courses which train missionaries and mission leaders among the Bhilstribe in Gujarat. Preparation of course materials by ABS faculty focuses on the needs of the people whic is important to revitalize the mission.

(iii) The role of Bishop R.B. Lal is very significant in the revitalization process of the mission of ABS. Hinduism, as a religion, is united with the stories, myths and temples mainly centered on the state of Uttar Pradesh. Allahabad is one of the major epicenters of Hinduism. In this epicenter, God raised a movement called Yesu Darbar under the leadership of Bishop R. B. Lal, Vice-Chancellor of the Sam Higginbottom Institute of Agriculture, Technology and Sciences (SHIATS, Deemed University) and President of the Association of Indian Universities. This movement spread out to almost the entire part of eastern Uttar Pradesh, some parts of Jharkhand, Bihar, Chhattisgarh, and Madhya Pradesh. God used this movement to clear the field and sow the seed in this region. Today, ABS mainly reaps what they have sown. Eight years ago, at one of the faculty retreats, Bishop Lal encouraged the ABS community to nuture the people who came to Christ with the work of Yesu Darbar.

(iv) In leadership, the role of Bishop Ezra Surgunam is also remarkable in the process of revitalizing the mission and vision of ABS.

(v) In addition, the contribution of a political movement is to be noted in preparing the field, among which the ABS church planting ministry is more concentrated. ABS always discerned the fact that, now, Uttar Pradesh is a harvest field of Christian mission; preparation of this harvest began during the 1970's with a subaltern movement, which revealed the age-old practices which held the majority Dalit communities under the umbrella of Hinduism. The political awakening of *Bahujan* (the majority community, mostly Dalits) paved the way for a spiritual awakening. Unlike other neighboring states, the *Bahujan* are not directly opposing the message of the Gospel, rather they are receptive to the gospel in Uttarpredesh. This particular situation is the outcome of this political shift. This political shift is the result of the *Bahujan* movement through their political outfit the Bhujan Samaj Party.

Theological/biblical truths through exploring ABS as a revitalization movement:

The following Biblical truths can be drawn from this case study:

(i) A biblical foundation in teaching students is important for authentic revitalization.

(ii) A commitment to the authority of scripture ought to be important for faculty, staff, and students. Hence, in the case of ABS, teaching evangelical theology based on Lausanne Covenant as an introductory theological course is important so that an evangelical basis may be formed in the students.

(iii) Reconciliation within the missional community (personal and collective) is vital to undertake authentic revitalization among target people groups. Reconciliation with God alone is not sufficient.

(iv) Strong prayer support for the leader both from within the family and outside.

(v) Full commitments to both male and female students to fulfill the complete call of God in their life. This means an inclusive approach of the leader towards people of various racial, ethnic, cultural, regional, linguistic, and gender backgrounds.

Next steps for leaders and scholars, both in their own actions and in the collective actions of which they are part:

(i) Sustaining the existing ministry and vision for the future leaders and the members of the mission organization.

(ii) To take the senior faculty members, other faculty, staff and board members into confidence along with their comments/reflections to ensure the implementation of the proposals gained from the conference.

(iii) Restatement of the vision and mission statements of the institute before the community. Occasional revisiting of the work done in the light of the vision and mission statement would enable keeping track of the growth process.

(iv) Provide opportunities for members of the team to grow academically, spiritually, and professionally.

(v) Nurturing of believers and catering to their needs in a more sensible manner should be done.

FUTURE

This case study has focused in detail on the factors that have contributed to the revitalization of ABS. The study has detailed the mission and vision and the major steps taken recently to focus more fully on revitalizing the vision of the founding fathers. In the process of the revitalization of Christian mission in North India, the following significant points can be drawn from this case study:

- Revitalization is possible through focusing on student/staff/ and faculty members personal spiritual growth.

- An multidenominational, inclusive composition of the community is beneficial.

- Restoring interpersonal relationships is key to help foster a positive team spirit and to form a cohesive group.

- Preference for a faculty with ministry experience.

- Very strong program for discipleship where students are mentored to model Christian character.

- Change in atmosphere with a positive willingness to accept change and a strong commitment to devotional commitments.

- Well-organized and effective field education with a unity of vision from board, students, and faculty.

- Strong foundation for academics with an evangelical conviction and a commitment to reconciliation and social justice ministries.

The study suggests the following points to improve and face the challenges of the future

- More frequent and efficient communication of the vision to stakeholders and community members.

- Re-examination of mission policies and practices time-to-time (may be twice a year).

- More intentional attempt to safeguard the evangelical foundation of the seminary. This case study thus brings out one of the revitalizing works of God in North India. Work of ABS also shows how God guides different people and organizations and knitting them together for the expansion of God's Kingdom in North India.

Case Study Four: Nepal Ebenezer Bible College

Ram Kumar Budhathoki, Yeshwanth B.V., B.P. Khanal

142 | CASE STUDY FOUR: NEPAL EBENEZER BIBLE COLLEGE

Abstract: This case study is to understand the work of God in and through the ministry of Nepal Ebenezer Bible College (NEBC) in its own socio-economic, cultural and ecclesial milieu and to find out the impacts the institute has made in transforming the lives of individuals and in the development of society at large. This study is done to find out whether the institute has been fulfilling its responsibility in serving the church and society. This study is basically an analytical study, which includes a brief understanding of its own historical background and context, its inception and development, and its ministry and motifs. Based on the analysis, we will find out in what manner the institute is contributing in revitalizing mission in Nepal today.

DEFINITION

To understand the context of Nepal Ebenezer Bible College, it is helpful to look at some historical factors of the country of Nepal. This information will help reveal how and why Christianity advanced rapidly despite many obstacles and much opposition.

The population of Nepal is very diverse, with more than one hundred different people groups and ethnicities with their own languages, dialects, and cultures. The vast majority of people were shaped by the Brahmanical social system, and the country remained the world's only Hindu kingdom until 2006. The religion of the land was imported from the Indian subcontinent and became the land of gods and goddesses from the earliest centuries in its history. For this reason, the country remained closed to "others" who might bring different religions, practices, or introduce a new way of life.

The earliest account of Christian missionary work in Nepal is credited to the Capuchin Fathers from Europe. Once they were driven out of Peking and Lhasa, they sought permission to stay in the Kathmandu valley. Some of the first Christians to settle in 1745 in Patan, one of the oldest towns in the valley, were those Capuchin missionaries.[48] Other groups of Capuchin missionaries later enter the valley and settled down in another town in the valley called Bhadgaun. They were able to win a handful of native Newars in Bhadgaon during their stay after

---

48 Makhan Jha, *The sacred complex of Kathmandu, Nepal: Religion of the Himalayan Kingdom* (New Delhi: Gyan Publishing House, 1995), 8f.

55 years,[49] but the mission did not last long. Shortly after King Prithvi Narayan Shah occupied the Kathmandu valley in 1768, his royal officers expelled 57 native Newari Christians from Bhadgaon (present day Bhaktapur) because they suspected that they might spy for the British in India.[50] That incident promoted the closed-door policy for Western missionaries and all Christian attempts for more than 200 years. Foreigners were not allowed even to visit Nepal until 1951.[51]

While Christianity was not welcome in Nepal, missionary zeal and compassion pioneered the planting of churches among immigrant Nepalese in the North-Eastern Indian states of Assam, Manipur, Meghalaya, Darjeeling, Sikkim, and Nagaland, and in the nations of Bhutan, and Burma as well. Many Nepalese migrated to different parts of India to work and support their families. Some would send their earnings back home and others chose to migrate with their whole family. Missionary efforts included medical centers and hospitals to penetrate Nepali speaking areas and people groups. Both missionaries and local Indian churches started mission efforts to share the gospel among the Nepalese. Hundreds of Nepalese churches were initiated and established in the Northern States of India, Burma and Bhutan, and around the bordering Indian cities.[52]

Even with the openness of multi-party democracy in 1951, the country remained closed not just to Christianity, but to any activities that would not favor the Panchayati government, until 1991. However, some early Christian work began in the early period of democracy, which witnessed the new life in Christ in many towns and villages throughout the country. Ramghat Church, the first evangelical church in Nepal, was planted in Pokhara in 1953, and two other churches started in the Kathmandu valley within the following year.[53] The church in Nepal experienced severe persecution in this period, yet in those thirty years of active monarchist

---

49 Jonathan Lindell, *Nepal and the Gospel of God*. Kathmandu: The United Mission to Nepal & Pilgrims Book House, 1997; p 30-31.
50 Cindy Perry, *A Biographical History of the Church in Nepal*. Kathmandu: Nepal Church History Project, 1990 (3rd Edition 2000), p 8f.
51 Rishikesh Shah, *An Introduction to Nepal*. Kathmandu: Ratna Pustak Bhandar, 1974, p 84.
52 Kiran Das, "The Growth of Christianity in Nepal". An article by, Bible Living Ministries Inc.; accessed from http://www.biblelivingministries.org/nepal_missions on 5th May 2013.
53 BP Khanal, *Amruwali Kanchho: A Biography of Pastor Tir Bahadur Dewan* (Nepali). Kathmandu: Samdan Publications, 1998, p 34.

single-party democracy, the church grew at a rapid rate underground, totaling more than 120 churches throughout the country.[54]

Until 1990, the country observed a closed-door policy in terms of religion and cultural exchanges, excluding other faiths and officially marginalizing all practices except Hinduism. It was unthinkable to evangelize in the country by any means. Preaching of the Gospel in public or even in private was not allowed. Missionary attempts to share the Gospel and distribute literature were threatened. After the single party system was defeated in 1991, the work of evangelization started openly in Nepal. The door was slightly opened to foreign missionaries to help initially develop schools, hospitals, industries, skill development and entrepreneurship training centers, community services and hydro-electricity.[55] It was an answer to prayer because many Churches and missionaries from other countries were praying for Nepal. Numbers of missionaries came into the country and began to work, along with a few pioneering native missionaries such as David Mukhiya, Buddhi Sagar Gautam, Tir Bahadur Dewan, Robert Karthak, Barnabas Rai, Daud Masih, and others who did very significant work in Nepal for the propagation of the Gospel.

Few churches were established by the mission agencies, since bilateral agreements with the government prevented missionaries from preaching the gospel or serving as religious clergy. No expatriate pastors served in Nepali congregations. The majority of the churches in these initial stages began as indigenous attempts by Nepali believers who started gathering for prayer, Bible study, fellowship, and worship. The credit for early church growth should go to the Nepalese Diaspora, particularly from the North Indian states, and the migrant Nepalese workers and soldiers in the Indian/British army who encountered Christ in different parts in India and brought the message to their love ones in Nepal. In this light, the Ghurkhas (Nepalese employees to the Indian and British armies) also played an important role of bringing the gospel to Nepal.

Despite the significant presence of a small numbers of denominations such as the Assemblies of God, the pre-1990 church in Nepal does not project an understanding of Western or Indian denominationalism. Christians in the minority

---

54 BP Khanal, *Prithak Bichar: Uncommon Thoughts on Contemporary Christian Leadership* (Nepali). Kathmandu: Bachan Books, 2012, p 192-201.
55 United Mission to Nepal (1954-2004), *Fifty Years in God's Hand: Blessings of the Past – Visions for the Future*. Kathmandu: United Mission to Nepal, 2004; p 94.

were struggling for their survival till 1990, rather than identifying themselves with their own theologies and denominations.

The Nepali Church as a whole is an indigenous phenomena with only the indirect involvement of foreign missionaries. Their role has been to challenge native Christians through their life-testimony and service by silently assisting those who accepted Christ and empowering them to carry on the task of evangelism and church planting. So, the Nepali church remains an indigenous movement.[56] However, foreign missionaries, Nepalese newly converted to Christianity, and job-seeking Christians from different parts of India began entering the open doors of Nepal since 1990. Until this time, the 120 churches of different denominational leanings were united as one church with only a few exceptions, such as the Assemblies of God and the Church of Christ. They were in one spirit of fellowship, praying together and sharing Christ by whatever means. But the new political changes of 1990 contributed towards an explosion of various denominations and groups, and even different sects and cults.[57] The national church leadership seemed drawn to these groups in order to access external resources, and many mission agencies worldwide seized the opportunity to start their own ministries in the country, which not only brought more resources but also different sects and denominations.

Norma Kehrberg, in her book, *The Cross in the Land of Khukuri* has listed some of the reasons that contributed to the recent rapid growth of Christianity in Nepal. According to her findings, the primary reasons a Nepali accepted Christ were: healing of self, healing of family, to receive salvation, to find peace, were struggling for their survival till 1990, rather than identifying themselves with their own theologies and denominations. The Nepali Church as a whole is an indigenous phenomena with only the indirect involvement of foreign missionaries. Their role has been to challenge native Christians through their life-testimony and service by silently assisting those who accepted Christ and empowering them to carry on the task of evangelism and church planting. So, the Nepali church remains an indigenous movement.[58] However, foreign missionaries, Nepalese newly converted to Christianity, and job-seeking Christians from different parts of India began entering the open doors of Nepal since 1990. Until this time, the 120 churches

---

56 Dr. Rajendra Rongong, *Early Churches in Nepal: An Indigenous Christian Movement Till 1990*. Kathmandu: Ekta Books, 2012, p 149.
57 BP Khanal, *Prithak Bichar*, p 196.
58 Dr. Rajendra Rongong, *Early Churches in Nepal: An Indigenous Christian Movement Till 1990*. Kathmandu: Ekta Books, 2012, p 149.

of different denominational leanings were united as one church with only a few exceptions, such as the Assemblies of God and the Church of Christ. They were in one spirit of fellowship, praying together and sharing Christ by whatever means. But the new political changes of 1990 contributed towards an explosion of various denominations and groups, and even different sects and cults.[59] The national church leadership seemed drawn to these groups in order to access external resources, and many mission agencies worldwide seized the opportunity to start their own ministries in the country, which not only brought more resources but also different sects and denominations.

Norma Kehrberg, in her book, *The Cross in the Land of Khukuri* has listed some of the reasons that contributed to the recent rapid growth of Christianity in Nepal. According to her findings, the primary reasons a Nepali accepted Christ were: healing of self, healing of family, to receive salvation, to find peace, to find truth, and as a family witness.[60] The majority of Christians in Nepal have come to Christ without missionary effort and they do not belong to any particular theological affiliation. These Christians make the church in Nepal unique in terms of being self-supporting, self-governing and self-propagating. Until 1990, Nepali churches resembled the first century church where churches were actively involved in bearing witnesses, healing, and performing miracles in the name of Jesus Christ without theological prejudices. One element that contributed the most is God's intervention through healings and miracles. Dr. Rajendra Rongong further highlights this fact, along with the important role of persecution, when he writes,

> Believers especially in rural and remote areas had a difficult time. Persecutions were rampant and sever. Not every instance of persecution is recorded. Yet the untold miseries made many of the simple and illiterate people very strong in their faith. Their faith and zeal confounded their interrogators. In some cases this happened to Christians even in city areas. Persecution gave birth to another encountering phenomenon. Wherever they were jailed, whether in urban of rural areas, believers shared the Gospel with their fellow inmates in prison. Prison and place or persecutions

---

59 BP Khanal, *Prithak Bichar*, p 196.
60 Norma Kehrberg, *The Cross in the Land of Khukuri*. Kathmandu: Ekta Books, 2002; p 137.

became their mission fields and many were converted through these ministries.[61]

Other reasons also attracted many people to the Christian faith. God revealed Himself through different times and occasions, and actively kept working in the lives of people, which opened the eyes of many to see who God is. Many were attracted to Christianity when they saw how Christians lived a life of peace, joy, love, and compassion, and how they modeled a life of true humility and service. The Christians' communal living, acceptance for all regardless of one's background, and balancing equality and mutual respect among themselves was also an attraction for many. A desire to live as equals with people from higher castes was another factor that drew many from the lower castes to Christianity. In addition, Christians typically had a progressive standard of living with an emphasis on good education, health and hygiene, and they maintained a high level of morality, discipline, and exemplary family life. These factors challenged others to put their faith in Christ Jesus as well. On the other hand, others sought deliverance from spiritual bondage, possession and sickness, as well as freedom from old tradition, caste-base social structures, costly rituals, customs and festivals, inequality and the gap between higher caste elites and the poor.

CONTEXT

By the end of the 1950's, with just a few scattered churches around the country, some leaders saw a growing need to gather isolated Christians together for fellowship. In 1960, a meeting was called in Bhaktapur, which eventually formed the Nepal Christian Fellowship (NCF), with the simple goal of giving encouragement and fellowship to the small groups of scattered churches and Christians. In 1992, the NCF Annual General Body Meeting changed its name to the National Churches Fellowship of Nepal (NCFN).

In their initial meeting in 1992, the NCFN outlined a number of key objectives. The first objective was to maintain spiritual unity among the churches. The second objective was to strengthen and encourage churches across Nepal by providing training, seminars, and conferences. The third objective was to facilitate and support evangelistic work and church planting. The fourth objective was to practically demonstrate the love of Christ through social services. To

---

61 Dr. Rajendra Rongong, p 103-4.

achieve these objectives, the NCFN formed five departments: the Theological Training Department, the Leadership Training Department, the Social Services Department, the Mission and Church-Planting Department and the Publication and Communication Department. Nepal Ebenezer Bible College (NEBC) was established as the theological training department of the NCFN in 1992 to address the pressing need for theologically trained pastors and leaders to serve in the rapidly growing Nepali Church. Currently NEBC is offering Bachelor of Theology—a three year course and Masters in Organizational leadership in partnership with Development Associates International.

NEBC is blessed with its own campus buildings. The main building has offices, classrooms, library, dormitories, kithchen, garden and multipurpose play ground. The other building is mainly for faculty. This inexpensive property is located in just five kilometers to the North-East from Kathmandu International Airport.

NEBC keeps regular contact with sponsoring churches or organizations through regular reports and newsletters, especially through email. They invite them as guest speakers in the chapel and invite them to the graduation ceremony. One unique feature of NEBC is that NEBC has a "weekend ministry program" through which students are sent to participate in ministry in the local churches. This enhances NEBC's relationship with the churches as it helps them to grow in maturity. NEBC also meets once a year with the churches where students are doing practical ministry. The institution has its own independent board to run the Bible College. However, in making major decisions, this board consults with the executive committee of National Churches Fellowship of Nepal (NCFN). Board members are also involved in the promotion of the institution based on their capacity. Some supervise, some raise funds, others teach or speak in the chapel. All of the administrative staff and faculty are encouraged to be actively involved in Church life. They are also encouraged to join the daily chapel, prayer retreat, and events organized by the institution where they are challenged to develop a heart for servant leadership.

The institution maintains a library with one full time staff member and six student assistants, and students are required to study in the library for at least four hours. Besides this college library, we also have the library of the ATEN (Association for Theological Education in Nepal) as an extended library, which is computerized. Students have access to 5,700 volumes of books in our college library and 18,600 books in the Library of ATEN. With 15% of the books written by Asian authors or related to the Asian context, the ATEN Library has a good collection of periodicals and journals, as well as books.

Spiritually, all staff members are expected to have a genuine born-again Christian experience and live a sound Christian life in practice. They are also expected to have a commitment to maintaining and promoting their evangelical faith and practice. Academically, all faculty, course writers, and tutors are expected to have a minimum of higher secondary education in general studies and a B.D./M. Div./M.A. in Biblical Studies, with ample experience of Christian ministry or an interrelated field. The duties of the academic department are to develop the course syllabus, upgrade the school curriculum to better equip the students, to involve students in practical and field ministry, to be in charge of the smooth functioning of the student discipleship groups, and handle issues related to student discipline.

From the birth of NEBC, the NCFN has played an important role in its development. The NCFN has given their best to develop NEBC's organizational structure, governance and administration, faculty, physical infrastructure, and to acquire goodwill from among the Nepali churches for NEBC. Its national and international networks have been great blessings for NEBC to both receive good students and also to enable the formation of mutual partnerships, which includes financial support, to carry out our mission for the Nepalese Church.

The vision of Nepal Ebenezer Bible College (NEBC) is to assist the Nepali Church in maturing into the fullness of Christ, so that it might transform the Christian community and society in Nepal. This is accomplished through its mission to build up servant-leaders with Christ-like character, rooted in scripture and equipped for holistic ministry. These aims are accomplished through three main institutional objectives: to prepare servant leaders with Christ-like character to serve church and society, to impart evangelical biblical teaching, and to impart ministerial skills to be meaningfully engaged in holistic mission.

The primary target group for NEBC is the Nepali Churches in Nepal and the Nepalese Diaspora. Some of our graduates are already working in India, Malaysia, Korea, Hong Kong, the Middle East, the USA, the Philippines, etc. We also accept Nepali students from India, especially West Bengal and North East India.

The ministry of NEBC focuses on academics as well as spiritual and ministerial areas. Academically, the institute emphasizes sound Biblical teaching and trains its pupil to be up-to-date with good theological understandings. It also trains its pupils to have a comprehensive understanding and the research skills needed to engage academic literature. This helps the students to be original in their research.

NEBC considers "spirituality" to be the backbone of the ministry. Hence, students are constantly mentored spiritually through daily devotions, chapel services, counseling groups such as the Agape Growth groups (AGG), fasting and whole night prayers.

With academics and spiritual formation, NEBC emphasizes ministry. The weekend ministry program serves this purpose. Students are required to participate in different church ministries. Every week ministry reports are to be submitted to the concerned authority in the college. This helps the students to develop skills for doing ministry in different set ups and conditions.

DEVELOPMENT

It is obvious that Nepal Ebenezer Bible College is not the only player in developing missions in Nepal, but part of a larger effort involving others. In recent years, there are dozens of Christian denominations, overseas mission agencies and movements active in missions through all kinds of means from evangelization, discipleship, church planting, and theological education. It can be said that the mainline denominations have started their own Bible training schools or colleges. Yet, NEBC stands in its original approach of being non-denominational and serving all Nepali churches at the maximum level possible. Being one of the oldest and most prominent Bible colleges in the country, NEBC has contributed the most towards Nepal mission in equipping young leaders in the past 22 years. The following paragraphs highlight some representative testimonies out of its 200 plus graduates:

Pastor Ananda Tamang's Testimony, Dolkha

It has been a great joy journeying with the Lord after the completion of my study at NEBC. Although I felt my call for the ministry when I was 13 years old, I could not truly grasp what it would look like before I came to NEBC. It was a huge privilege to be trained under dedicated leaders of the Word. It was the teaching and inspiration of those leaders of the Word that helped my vision and call to be polished for the lost and the rural villages. I am so thankful to God for bringing me into contact with a few people who have so impacted my life and ministry, especially shaping me for the battlefield after my studies.

It was not easy while I was studying, but God never left me alone. He helped me courageously and successfully complete the study at NEBC under the guidance and counsel of committed faculty members, who, as I believe were led and filled by the Holy Spirit to impact others. After the completion of my studies, I decided to work as a tentmaker in Charikot, Dolakha, where I served the Lord in a local church, and worked in a private school to support myself. With the financial situation, I had to fly to Doha and take a job abroad for two years. It was a good job, but I was always reminded of my calling, and this made my heart restless. It was God's sovereign plan to bring me to the Nepalese Church; I believe the largest in the diaspora, with more than 1000 believers in Qatar with multiple congregations all over Qatar. God allowed me to serve in the church in the pastorate for more than 20 months, where I was responsible for the teaching and preaching of the Word, and for evangelism and worship. It was a great honor to see many people saved, baptized, and growing in the Lord. In my last days there, I had more responsibilities added as I began to think that I would be the future lead pastor of the church. But my heart was not truly enjoying what I was doing. I had a great job and the opportunity of leading many to Christ was important, as well as teaching and discipling, but my heart was looking for something else.

I came back to Nepal for a vacation in October 2007, to spend time with my family and home church in the village, but God had another plan for me. Right after my return from Doha, He took me to Jiri. I had served for one year in the nearby city of Charikot, but never planned to go to Jiri, but God planned for me to be there. God started to show me the needs there, and I was directly and indirectly responding to what God was showing me through my trips to the villages, speaking with leaders and ordinary believers. It was truly difficult for me to work there for the first three years without any salary or support. I am so thankful for the leaders like Pastor Gyan Bahadur Sunuwar and Pastor Shakti Tamang, who generously helped me financially when I had to come to see my family. So, I started to work again as a tent making minister, teaching the English language to college students, nurses, workers in the financial sector, and even the Head Masters of high schools. That did not support me sufficiently, but God provided for my needs. From the beginning of November, I started to teach at the Bible School, which is currently under my leadership, and we started a church in Jiri praying for it to become a model church. It is a difficult society in Jiri, so we wanted to preserve our Christian testimony to bring glory to God and reach out to those who had not heard the gospel. We started the church with less than 15 local believers, including a newborn baby. I was impatient at times because sometimes not even one person would come to the church, but God prompted us in our hearts to pray. God gradually brought growth to the church. After six years or so, I am surprised to see how God has brought about this growth in His church.

Now I pastor a local church with two congregations, Jiri Christian Church, and by God's grace we have started a new church in a nearby village in January of 2014. The burden in my heart is to build the church, especially in the rural areas of Nepal. One thing that breaks my heart is when I see a bunch of churchgoers who have the wrong view of Jesus. We are happy to hear and read that Nepal has the fastest growing church in the world. That is great. But have you ever thought about the large chance that many misguided people in the church might still miss the chance to enter heaven? I am not the one who will judge, but this is something serious that we need to think about. For this reason, we have launched church-based training in the villages, with a vision of building strong and healthy churches. I want to see all churchgoers in heaven.

By God's grace, I have been leading an indigenous ministry organization called Himalayan United Christian Fellowship of Nepal for more than half a decade, where the local churches in the Himalayas come together for prayer, worship, and edification, regardless of their denomination. It is another privilege that I can invest in the young people that are becoming the new church leaders for our growing churches through the leadership training that I have been leading for the past five years. If you desire to see all churchgoers in heaven, then it is important that you multiply people who can bring the gospel message to the unreached areas and teach people at the church level.

One thing that God has put in my heart is to develop leaders around me who can take leadership in times of need. However developing people has not been easy so far. But it is God's church and he will bring people to us that will faithfully serve Him and His church. I believe God has enabled me to do this at some level and I am so thankful for what God has been doing. At the same time, I am glad that I could recruit and mobilize the Ebenezer graduates with me to carry out the Great Commission to the Himalayas.

Pastor Navaraj Pandey, Nawalparasi

After finding my calling to full-time pastoral ministry while I was in the final years of my B.Th., I started serving this church as its pastor in 2000. Since then, by God's grace, I have been trying my best to bring glory to God by mainly working in three areas. First, by working in pastoral ministry and church planting, we have been able to plant five churches, which have altogether 300 baptized members, by 2013. Second, in equipping the church, with the help of neighboring churches, my church ran three sessions of the "Bible Training Center for Pastors" training. We have 70 graduates from this program. We also have a Paul- Timothy Training program with 30 graduates. On top of this, my church leaders and I have been doing personal discipleship and mentoring to select church members.

Third, we have been working in the area of social services. As the chairperson of the Local Christian Society (*Isai Samaj Nawalparasi*), I have been heavily involved in helping the community. In partnership with nongovernmental and governmental organizations, we run a literary course for people in the church and community. Once they are literate and interested in more training, then we give what is called a "Functional Course." In this course, the participants learn skills for generating income, like vegetable farming, poultry raising, making soap, handicrafts, and more. We also help direct them to those NGOs or INGOs who are working to help people acquire skills for better living. The Church Community Mobilization Program (CCMP) is another important program we are doing for our community and society at large. First, we give training to church members on how to analyze the community in identifying the primary needs of that community, to explore the available human and other resources available at the local level, and finally to mobilize it for the development of the community. Through this program, the community has been mobilized to successfully complete and sustain a drinking water project, run their literacy programs, etc.

Khim Kumari Kunwar, Pokhara

I am Khim Kumari Kunwar from Pokhara, Nepal, and I am one of the B.Th. graduates from Nepal Ebenezer Bible College (NEBC) who finished in 2010. After my graduation, I returned to my village and engaged in ministry in my own church as one of the leaders. By God's grace, I am now working as an Integral Mission Trainer Facilitator in a Para-church organization called *Sagol*. I am also continuing to minister in the Youth and Women's fellowship at my local church.

Integral Mission is demonstrating God's love by words and deeds in the community. Every church should be involved in Integral Mission. As a training facilitator, I teach about holistic missions and programs among the Nepalese churches, Bible colleges, and Christian organizations. We organize the programs in partnership with the churches and local communities to empower them and to fulfill the Great Commission of Jesus Christ through our actions. The understanding and knowledge I gained about God, God's Word, and the people in the NEBC has helped me to be an effective Integral Mission Training Facilitator.

In this era, the Church must show the love of God by being involved in social and community work. The distribution of gospel tracts, pamphlets, and Bibles is good but aided with a practical demonstration of God's love makes it easier to fulfill the Great Commission. Finally, I pray that all of us, Christian brothers and sisters, pastors and leaders, will be able to demonstrate our faith through action. May God help us to love our neighbors as ourselves!

Pastor Harihar Chaudhari, Banke (from his ministry report)

Another alumnus of NEBC Harihar Chaudhari, now works as a full-time pastor in Banke district, in the Mid-Western Region. After graduation he returned to his own place and started a school and is contributing towards his community's development. His innovative work, pioneering an entrepreneurship approach of mission-ministry works. His initiative of generating income help for his discipled-leaders and church members allowed them to create some sort of livelihood for themselves. For this purpose, he started fishery and poultry-raising projects.

On the other hand, Harihar actively takes leadership in training pastors, and has started a six-month training program, which has been championing the church planting work in the region as a movement. He also initiated schools for children and adult education and literacy programs. His church ministries and active leadership roles in wider social issues has earned much credit unto the Lord Jesus Christ.

Practices

The institution believes in the theory of balancing life inside and outside the classroom, and has been continuously working on ways to mold our students with knowledge, skills, and the proper attitude (behavior). The courses were designed to keep our students engaged in class and the library on one hand, and the chapel, group fellowships, social activities, different contests, sports, and field ministries on the other. The institution requires every student to share the gospel to at least ten non-believers every semester, and by the time they graduate they should have made at least five disciples. Also, the institution assigns each student a weekend ministry in a church in the valley where they are exposed to practical ministry during the three years of their study at NEBC. The activities they are involved in at the churches include preaching, Bible study, house fellowship, youth meeting, choir, Sunday school, women's fellowship, etc. NEBC highly emphasizes character formation and the healthy relational development of every student. To achieve this purpose, the institution has divided students into different discipleship groups called Agape Growth Groups, where a group of students is assigned to a teacher who helps them develop in their Christian life.

NEBC's ministry can be evaluated in three categories, which are academic, spiritual, and ministerial. Academically, NEBC concentrates on students' academic development with it's well-structured syllabus. The syllabus has a well-balanced outlook in terms of theological, Biblical and practical subjects. This enables NEBC to fulfill its vision to develop potential servant-leaders for a holistic ministry. Spiritually, NEBC concentrates on the spiritual development of the students. This is done through mentoring by faculty. They have Agape Growth Groups (AGG), with a faculty mentor, where the students have the opportunity to share their problems and also grow spiritually. Besides this, NEBC has daily devotions early each morning. NEBC also has a devotion program through which students are encouraged to read Scriptures with an aim to complete the whole Bible in one year. Besides this they are also encouraged to write their reflections every day. Ministry wise, NEBC concentrates on the ministerial development of the students. This is done through "weekend ministry." Students are required to participate in church ministry every week. This enables them to develop their skills in church management and pulpit ministry. Besides this, the institution often conducts community development activities like cleaning the surrounding areas, and visiting some hospitals for the physically challenged, in order to counsel them. Therefore, students are trained for a holistic ministry for the revitalization of missions in Nepal.

NEBC with it's inter-denominational dimension, coupled with its concern for the Nepalese church at large, has been impacting the churches since its inception. One of the main motifs behind its creation was the development of church leadership. This vision was realized and appropriated well in its academic and ministerial programs in training students.

The weekend ministry of the institution is instrumental in impacting local churches. The students are required to go to different churches and help the church leadership in its management and pulpit ministry. Later on, these churches take these students to continue the work of the church. In this way, churches are provided potential well-trained leaders with a servant-leadership attitude.

LEARNINGS

In the light of this study, it was found that the NEBC has to work in a pluralistic society. Cindy Perry points out that Nepal is a "mosaic of diverse cultures, languages, ethnic groups and religious practices."[62] Dr. Mangal Man Maharjan on Nepal, with C. V. Matthew points out that Hinduism, which is the major religion of the state, constitutes 89% of the population.[63] However, this 89% is a matter of suspicion for scholars with the rising view of ethnic consciousness among different tribes in Nepal.[64] Nevertheless, in this context the church is constantly challenged for its existence. It is in this context, that NEBC shares the burden with the church to address the challenges for its existence. It has always been difficult to communicate the Gospel in the multi-religious context of Nepal. Therefore, the church has used social action as a means to communicate the Gospel initially. In fact, the critiques of Christianity opine that it was because of this social and missionary service, that

---

62   Cindy Perry, "Nepal," ed. Scott W. Sunquist, *A Dictionary Asian Christianity*, Grand Rapids, MI: William B. Eerdmans Publishing Company, 2001, p 593.
63   C. V. Matthew with Mangal Man Maharjan on Nepal, "Hindusim," ed. Scott W. Sunquist, *A Dictionary Asian Christianity*, Grand Rapids, MI: William B. Eerdmans Publishing Company, 2001, p. 334–335.
64   C. V. Matthew with Mangal Man Maharjan, "Hindusim," 334; and Perry, "Nepal," p 593.

the conversion and adoption of Christianity has been taking place.⁶⁵ Therefore, we see a dichotomy between the evangelical mandate and the social mandate of the gospel. Though Western theologies in principle have been helpful, they have not been fully able to communicate the Gospel in a comprehensible way at the practical and existential levels.

Therefore, it is found that there is a need for the Nepalese church to articulate its faith in a way that is comprehensible to a Nepali without losing its Christian essence. It is also true that the Gospel should not be dichotomized between evangelism and social work, but it should be presented with a proper balance.

The nature of the work is missional. It is found that NEBC strikes a harmonious balance between the social mandate and the evangelical mandate in carrying out missions. The impact of this aspect can be seen in its commitment to teach and train students to be well-grounded in the Scriptures and in its concern for community development. This is carried out first, by regularly conducting classes and seminars for academic development. Second, through spiritual mentoring, where students' character and spiritual life is shaped. Third, through theological praxis, where students are inspired and challenged to serve the needs of the community. For this, a number of social analytical subjects have been developed. For the institution such as peace and reconciliation (The Micah Network), integral missions (UMN), a Christian response to HIV/ AIDS, counseling on subjects like ministry for the youth, children and ministry, and seminars on subjects like the role of women in church and society.

The impact of the work is very dynamic. First, the churches are provided with potential leaders with a servant–leadership attitude. This will ensure better church management and also sound biblical teaching in the church. Second, NGO's and INGO's are benefiting through the skills acquired by students in their training. This will ensure better contributions for the development of the community at large. Third, missional fields are provided ample missionaries. Students are well trained to do missions in a meaningful way. This will ensure better results on the mission field. Fourth, the diaspora ministry of the Nepalese church has also benefitted. Some of the students are serving in the USA, the UK, Finland, Malaysia, India, Bhutan, and other places. This will ensure the growth of the Nepalese church outside the country of Nepal and also contribute to church growth in Southeast Asia at large.

---

65 Trilok Manjupuria and Rohit Kumar Manjupuria, *Religons in Nepal*. Kathmandu: M. Devi Lashkar (Gwalior), 2004, p 323.

It can be seen that NEBC has been successfully translating its vision and mission in its organizational, ministerial, and spiritual areas. Organizationally, we can see a well-established system of accountability under the supervision and involvement of the NCFN and the NEBC board. Ministry-wise, we can see a balanced outlook of evangelism and social service for a holistic impact. Spiritually, we can see an emphasis on Bible study, both by the staff and students with regular fasting and whole night prayers. Besides, this the institution is constantly concerned for community development. This aspect is very much evident in its participation in social service in terms of cleaning its surroundings, visiting orphanages, hospitals, and feeding street children. In this way, NEBC has been practicing and projecting Christ's love both in word and deed in its own context. This indeed, revitalizes the mission in Nepal.

FUTURE

Looking at the complex and multi-religious context of Nepal, it is always a challenge to communicate the Gospel. In this context, the means and ways of communicating the Gospel have been revitalized. It is not merely evangelism, or merely social service, but it is a harmonious synthesis of both. Looking at the diverse background of students in terms of their ethnicity, academic standard, and personal history, it has always been a challenge to teach and mentor holistically. The methods of teaching are revitalized in such a way that students benefit holistically in terms of academics, personality development, and ministry. Looking at the rapid growth of the church and its need for leaders, students must be trained in the skill of not just planting a church, but also helping the church to grow into a mature institution in terms of its organizational structure and spiritually.

The missional mandate for church–planting should be a "synthesis"[66] of missional imperative as proclamation of the Word and of social action in the contemporary world. There should be no dichotomized motif in planting the church. John Stott says that if we view it as a "... broader concept of mission as Christian service in the world comprising both evangelism and social action- a concept which is laid upon us by the model of our Savior's mission in the world- then Christians could under God make a far greater impact on society..."[67]

---

66   John Stott, *Christian Mission In the Modern World*. Downers Grove, IL: Inter-Varsity Press, 1975, p 20.
67   Ibid., p 34.

A synthesis is presupposed here. A synthesis between the social mandate and the evangelical mandate should be imbibed in the Church's role to carry missions in the contemporary world. There has to be a "convergence of conviction"[68] as David J. Bosch puts it. The role of the church can also be understood in Paul S. Minear who says, "... the church received its being on the battle-line where it received its mandate."[69] We can also see this synthesis of word and deed in the Bible. The prophetic mandate of the Old Testament presupposes spirituality and need for social responsibility (Micah 6: 6-8). In the New Testament, the great commission involves a social responsibility as Jesus stands as a paradigm of this synthesis.

Paul S. Minear categorizes the role of the Church under nine headings- "Preaching, healing, testimony before governors and Kings, peace-making, the breaking of bread and prayers, teaching, scriptural interpretation, 'whatever you do,' 'we rejoice in our suffering'..."[70] With these nine functions of the church, Paul S. Minear also creates a synthesis of word and deed. There is a need to rethink and rearticulate the role of the church based on the Biblical synthesis of *kerygma* and *diakonia* in its responsibility to carry out missions in the contemporary world. First, this synthesis should be a Christo-centric synthesis as Jesus presents a model of this blend. Second, the church should reflect this synthesis in her witness, evangelism and service in the contemporary world.

Given the pluralistic context of the church in Nepal, the church should renovate its role and discern how, when, and in what way she needs to proclaim the Gospel. Therefore the synthesis of the word and deed in the role of the church calls for the unity of the churches, to encourage her members to be better witnesses in the world at large, the need of innovative ways of evangelism, and to instill in her members the need for social action. Therefore, the synthesis of *kerygma* and *diakonia* in the role of the church will optimize her relevance in the contemporary world. Keeping this in mind, the missional mandate for church–planting should be a synthesis of *kerygma* and *diakonia*. Only then, can the church holistically revitalize the society.

---

68 David J. Bosch, *Transforming Mission Paradigm Shift in Theology of Mission*. Maryknoll, New York: Orbis, p 511.
69 Paul Sevier Minear, "Vocation of the church: some exegetical clues". *Missiology* 5, no. 1 (January 1, 1977): 26.
70 Minear, pp 5:27-29.

The theological motif for a missional mandate as synthesis of *kerygma* and *diakonia* has been helping the institution to meaningfully contextualize the Gospel. This contextualization is not just in terms of evangelism but also in its social service. This aspect can be seen in its programs like the Gospel music program, which is evangelical in nature, and feeding street children, cleaning neighboring areas and visiting hospitals for physically challenged. The churches are provided with potential and well-informed leaders with a strong biblical foundation, good spiritual maturity and a love for service.

One way of understanding the relationship between the theology and ministry of NEBC in this study is by the way of seeing it as "contextualizing" the gospel. The study also reveals that the institute quickly saw that the inadequacy of Western theologies, though helpful in principle, was that they were not fully able to communicate the Gospel. Therefore, the institute felt the need to articulate its Christian faith in a way that is comprehensible by a Nepali. The institute also realized that a one-sided evangelism will not bring about the revitalization of mission in Nepal. Therefore, it opted for a holistic approach to impact both the church and society. This contextualization is biblically–oriented, both exegetical and practical. In other words, the Word of God is carefully exegeted in its own Biblical context and then applied to the Nepali context in order to be transformed or revitalized. It is in this context, that ministry is nothing but theology in action.

In terms of the long-term development of a Christian academic program, the experience of NEBC has shown the need for several crucial steps. First, it is important to develop the infrastructure with modern facilities for the effective training of students and to provide a comfortable atmosphere for research. Second, it is essential to develop full–time faculty who can teach and mentor students on campus. Third, it is important to develop library resources for research, and finally, work to upgrade the institution to the Master's level.

For important long-term trends, it is a major expectation for the future that the church and seminaries should work more closely together in solidarity to create opportunities for both training students practically and placing graduates in ministry. This will ensure the growth and maturation of young theologians in the mission field. There is no point in producing graduates every year without having adequate opportunities for them to use their ministry skills. In order to accomplish this, church, religious organizations, and seminaries should work hand–in–hand.

Another long-term goal is the developing of a unique "Nepalese Christian Theology." Nepal has its own distinct context, and often, Western theologies are not able to address the existential struggles of the Nepalese church. Therefore, the Nepalese church, including its seminaries, need to articulate the Christian faith in a way which is biblically oriented, but also completely natural in the Nepalese context.

There are two key concepts that stand out in discussing the realization of these long-term trends and goals. One is partnership and the other is participation. These goals cannot be achieved without the institution's partnership with the local church and other organizations (both NGO's and INGO's). However, this partnership can only work to the extent that we participate in common goals. Participation is the common sharing of the burden for community development. In this way, through participation with partners with shared goals and vision, the institution can actively take part in the revitalization of mission in Nepal. Besides partnership and participation, there is another key concept ... preparation. NEBC is committed to prepare theologians, servant-leaders, who can articulate a Christian faith relevant to the Nepalese context. To realize these goals, solidarity between churches, para-church organizations, and seminaries has to be envisioned. The realization of this vision will create ministerial opportunities for budding ministers and young theologians.

Through NEBC's inception, development and its ministry, one can see how God is using this institution to revitalize mission in Nepal. NEBC has been a major contributor in coping with the challenges encountered by the churches in Nepal. Bringing the light of the gospel to the lives of millions and inspiring churches to be a catalyst for social transformation, NEBC plays a role as a coach beyond the academic playground. There are hundreds of first generation Christian leaders who have received missionally practical training from NEBC and are active in the mission field, most of them leading churches as pastors throughout Nepal or with the Nepalese diaspora. NEBC should always strive to seek new avenues for doing ministries in its ever-changing world. It should never deviate from its scriptural foundation and gospel mandate. This will ensure the continuity of the revitalization of mission in Nepal.

Theological Evaluation of NEBC Ministry

NEBC's ministry can be evaluated under three aspects: academic enhancement, spiritual development and ministry efficiency. Academically, NEBC does concentrate on students' academic development with its contextually well-structured syllabus. The syllabus has a well-balanced outlook in terms of theological, Biblical and practical subjects in local-national context. This enables NEBC to fulfill its vision to develop potential servant-leaders for a wholistic ministry. Spiritually, NEBC focuses on the spiritual formation and development of the students. This is done through mentoring by faculty. They do have Agape Growth Group (AGG) in which a faculty will be assigned to some students where the students have the opportunity to share their problems and also it is a place where they grow spiritually. Besides AGG, NEBC has a strict routine of daily devotions early each morning. NEBC also has devotion program through which students are encouraged reading Scriptures with an aim to complete the whole Bible in one year. Besides this they are also encouraged to write their reflections every day. Ministerially, NEBC does concentrate on ministerial development of the students. This is done through 'weekend ministry.' Students are required to participate in church ministry every week. This enables them to develop their skills in church management and pulpit ministry. Besides this, the institution often conducts community development activities like cleaning the surrounding areas, and some hospitals for the physically challenged in order to counsel them. Therefore, students are holistically trained for a holistic ministry for the vitalization of missions in Nepal.

Theological Evaluation for a Holistic Impact

The above theological evaluation of NEBC ministries gives us an idea of the institution's impact on church and society is what aimed for. The holistic approach in training students has been enabling the institution to impact church and society in a very dynamic way. The theological motif for a missional mandate as the synthesis of kerygma and diakonia has been helping the institution to meaningfully contextualize the Gospel in a meaningful way. This contextualization is not just in terms of evangelism but also in its social service. This aspect can be seen in its programs like the Gospel musical program, which is evangelical in nature, and feeding street children, cleaning neighboring areas, and visiting hospitals for the physically challenged. The churches are provided with potential and well-informed leaders with a strong biblical foundation, good spiritual maturity, and love for service.

Final Evaluation

Finally, the practical theological approach that is employed by NEBC is a holistic approach. The case study reveals that the institute has a very good theological praxis in which it synthesized evangelism and social service in a harmonious way. It is very much evident in how the institute took pains to relate theology and its ministry, which we will discuss below.

Relationship between theology and ministry of NEBC

One way of understanding the relationship between theology and ministry of NEBC in this study is by the way of seeing it as "contextualizing" the gospel. The study also reveals that the institute quickly saw the inadequacy of western theologies though helpful in principle, was not fully able to communicate the Gospel. Therefore, the institute felt the need to articulate its Christian faith in a way it is comprehensible by a Nepali. The institute also realized that a one-sided evangelism will not bring about vitalization of mission in Nepal. Therefore, it opted for a holistic approach as contextualization of the Gospel for the holistic impact on church and society. This contextualization is biblically oriented i.e., to say exegetical and practical. In other words, the Word of God is carefully exegeted in its own biblical context and then applied to the Nepali context in order to be transformed or vitalized. It is in this context, ministry is nothing but theology is action.

Impact of other churches

NEBC with its inter-denominational dimension coupled with its concern for the Nepali church at large has been impacting the churches since its inception. One of the main motifs behind the inception is for the development of the church leadership. This vision was realized and appropriated well in its academic and ministerial programs in training students. The weekend ministry of the institution is instrumental in impacting the churches. The students are required to go to different churches and help the church leadership in its management and pulpit ministry. Later on, these churches take these students to continue the work in the church. In this way, churches are provided potential and well-trained leaders with servant- leadership attitude. Some alumni are working with Nepali church overseas. They are also contributing towards the Diaspora Nepali church growth.

Effects of vitalization of mission

The institute's holistic approach towards ministry and its synthesis of evangelism and social service has indeed been effecting the vitalization of mission in Nepal. The vitalization of mission through NEBC can be categorized into two – ecclesial and societal. With regard to the former, NEBC shaped and molded potential servant-leaders for the growing church of Nepal. This in turn enabled the Nepali church to contribute to the vitalization of mission in Nepal locally and internationally. With regard to the later, the institute has developed good will with the neighbors through its social work. Besides this, the institute's relationship with NGO's likes UMN and Micah also enhanced the effect of vitalization of mission in Nepal.

Necessary Steps in the Future

New Orientation: New Steps

The case study provided not only an introspective – retrospective analysis but also it helped to realize new orientations that should be made. The new steps that are to be considered are firstly, developing the infrastructure with modern facilities for an effective training of the students and a comfortable atmosphere for research. Secondly, developing full-time faculty who can teach and mentor students on campus. Thirdly, developing library resources for the research. Fourthly, upgrading the institution to Master's level.

Expectations for the future

The major expectation for the future is that the church and seminaries should have solidarity in working together and creating opportunities for the graduates. This will ensure the growth and maturing of young theologians in the mission field. It is no point producing graduates every year without adequate opportunities for them. In order to accomplish this, church, organizations and seminaries should work hand–in–hand.

Another expectation is to develop 'Nepal Christian Theology.' Nepal has its own distinct and unique context. Western theologies are not able to address the existential struggles of the Nepali church. Therefore, the Nepali church including seminaries, should seek to articulate the Christian faith in a contextual way which is biblically oriented.

Realization of the expectations

There are three key words that stand out in discussing the realization of the expectations. They are partnership, participation, and preparation. The realization is done through the institute's partnership with the local church, organizations, other Bible colleges, NGO's and INGO's. NEBC should be always open to partner with other institutions to revitalize the missions in Nepal. The partnership comes to fruition through participation. Participation is sharing the burden for community development. In this way, the institute can actively take part in vitalization of mission in Nepal. This is very much evident in the testimonies given by some of the alumnus who are involved in integral missions in Nepal and also in diaspora Nepali churches. Besides these two key words there is one more i.e., preparing. The institute is committed to prepare theologians, servant-leaders who can articulate a Christian faith relevant to Nepali context. To realize the mentioned expectations, solidarity between churches, Para-churches and seminaries has to be envisioned. The realization of this vision will create ministerial opportunities for the budding ministers and young theologians.

Conclusion

This case study explored how NEBC contributed towards revitalization of missions in Nepal. This exploration helped us to remember the beginnings, growth and development of NEBC. NEBC along with the Nepali church had to struggle for its existence in its pluralistic society. Though the church was struggling for its existence, it was growing rapidly. To bring solidarity between these growing churches the National Churches Fellowship of Nepal was born in 1960. The focus of this organization is to provide spiritual leadership to all the churches. To accomplish this objective NCFN felt the need to train pastors and leaders. NEBC was born to fulfill this need. NEBC's mission is to build servant–leaders with Christ-like character, deeply rooted in Scripture, equipped for holistic ministry. Since, its inception NEBC has been striving to fulfill this mission to see the Nepali church matured into the fullness of Christ. This vision and mission has been well translated into its practical life in terms of its organizational structure, relationship with churches, involvement of the board and NCFN, faculty and academics. The fruition of NEBC's ministry can be seen in the lives and ministries of its alumni. NEBC's alumni are not only contributing to the local church, but also to the diaspora church of Nepal. The contributions are not only confined to ecclesial context but to the society at large. Hence, NEBC is contributing and continuing the Gospel mandate holistically.

The study also helped to envision new steps for further development of theological education and maturity of the church. A better infrastructure, library resources and qualified faculty will ensure a healthy development of theological education. Theologically, new steps towards a biblically oriented contextualization are needed in order to articulate a Christian faith that can address the existential struggles of the Nepali Church and society at large. Future expectations can be seen in the solidarity between the churches and para-church organizations for holistic ministry and dynamic church growth. The realization of this expectation will ensure ample opportunities for an increasing number of graduates to exercise what they have studied in the seminaries. This will contribute to the revitalization of missions in Nepal in a very dynamic manner.

Therefore, by looking at NEBC's inception, development, and its ministry one can see how God is using this institute to revitalize mission in Nepal. NEBC should always strive to seek new avenues in doing ministry with an ever-changing world around it. It should never deviate from its Scriptural foundation and Gospel mandate. This will ensure the continuity of revitalization of mission in Nepal.

Works Cited

Bista, Dor Bahadur
    1991   *Fatalism And Development: Nepal's Struggle for Modernization.* Kolkata, India: Orient Longman.

Bosch, David J.
    2006   *Transforming Mission Paradigm Shift in Theology of Mission.* Edited by Siga Arles. First Indian edition. Missiological Calssics Series 1. Bangalore, India: Centre for Contemporary Christianity.

Das, Kiran
    n.d.   *The Growth of Christianity in Nepal.* An article by Bible Living Ministries Inc.; accessed from http://www.biblelivingministries.org/nepal missions on 5th May 2013.

Jha, Makhan
    1995   *The Sacred Complex of Kathmandu.* Nepal: Religion of the Himalayan Kingdom (New Delhi, India: Gyan Publishing house).

Kehrberg, Norma
    2002   *The Cross in the Land of Khukri.* Kathmandu, Nepal: Ekta books.

Khanal, B.P.
    1998   *Amrwali Kancho: A Biography of Pastor Tir Bahadur Dewan.* Kathmandu, Nepal: Samdan publications.

    2012   *Prithak Bichar (Uncommon Thoughts on Contemporary Christian Leadership).* Kathmandu, Nepal: Bachan books.

Lindell, Jonathan
    1997   *Nepal And the Gospel of God.* Kathmandu: The United Mission to Nepal & Pilgrims books house.

Manjupuria, Trilok, and Rohit Kumar Manjupuria
    2004   *Religions in Nepal.* Kathmandu, Nepal: M. Devi Lashkar (Gwalior).

Matthew, C. V., with Mangal Man Maharjan
    2001   "Hindusim." Edited by Scott W. Sunquist. *A Dictionary Asian Christianity*. Grand Rapids, MI: William B. Eerdmans Publishing Company.

Minear, Paul Sevier
    1977   "Vocation of the Church: Some Exegetical Clues." *Missiology* 5(1): 13–37.

Perry, Cindy
    2000   *A Biographical History of the Church in Nepal*. Third edition. Kathmandu, Nepal: Nepal Church History Project.

    2001   "Nepal," edited by Scott W. Sunquist. *A Dictionary Asian Christianity*. Grand Rapids, MI: William B. Eerdmans Publishing Company.

Raj Baral, Lok
    1997   *Oppositional Politics in Nepal*. New Delhi, India: Abhinav publications.

Rongong, Rajendra
    2012   *Early Churches in Nepal: An Indigenous Christian Movement Till 1900*. Kathmandu, Nepal: Ekta.

Shah, Rishikesh
    1974   *An Introduction to Nepal*. Kathmandu, Nepal: Ratna Pustak Bhandar.

Stott, John
    1975   *Christian Mission In the Modern World*. Downers Grove, IL: Inter-Varsity Press.

United Mission to Nepal (1954 – 2004)
    2004   *Fifty Years in God's Hand: Blessing of the Past –Visions for the Future*. Kathmandu, Nepal: United Mission to Nepal.

Case Study Five: Native Missionary Movement

Principal Researchers: Finny Philip, Ph.D, Abraham Cherian, Ph.D, Erik Disch
Written By: Erik Disch

Abstract: The native Missionary Movement was birthed in the "post-colonial Indian context." There was a strong anti-Christian attitude, due in large part to the connection between Christianity and the colonialists. At the same time, the emerging Pentecostal movement in South India, particularly in Kerala, was producing a zeal for missions. It was this zeal that had prompted Thomas Mathews to travel to Rajasthan and start his gospel work. The native Missionary Movement is understood best within the context of the ministries that serve as an extension of its vision. The NMM has focused initiatives in church planting, education, health care, publishing and community development.

DEFINITION

In 1962, a young college student from South India heard the call of God for his life. In response to this call, Thomas Mathews committed his life to serve the Lord in "the hardest of mission fields:" North India. God had already miraculously saved his life from drowning when he was still a rebellious teenager, so there was no question in his mind that God would be with him now.

In April 1963, the Lord directed his steps to Udaipur, a small town in Rajasthan. Udaipur was relatively unknown at that time, but has since developed into a significant domestic and international tourist destination. Without a sending or supporting organization to back him, Thomas Mathews began what would turn out to be his life's work in a rented room, paying 15 rupees per month.

Although he faced much hardship early in his ministry, he remained faithful to the vision God had placed before him. He spent his early years in partial starvation, often facing persecution and severe beatings. He learned to rely heavily on the Lord to meet even his most basic daily needs. His example would serve as a model for those who came to serve along side him.[71]

By God's grace, Thomas baptized his first convert, a young Rajasthani man, in October 1964. This marked the beginning of the Rajasthan Pentecostal Church, an "Antioch" in North India.[72] In June 1966, he married Mary, a dedicated seminary student, who also shared his heart and vision for North India.

---

71 Abraham T. Cherian. "Contribution of Churches and Missions to the Bhils of Rajasthan". (PhD diss., Asia Institute of Theology, 2005).
72 RPC was first established as Filadelfia Church and just celebrated its 50 year Golden Jubilee in December 2013. The establishment of this church was the 'first fruits' of the Native Missionary Movement and many more church plants to come.

In January 1981, God spoke to Brother Mathews and a handful of his young, Rajasthani co-workers through a vision. They saw in the vision a particular geographical area touching Gujarat and Maharashtra states. They knew they were to go there, to "launch out into the deep" trusting the word that God had given them. They saw this as a "Macedonian" call (Acts 16:6-10) and they responded accordingly.

Upon reaching their destination, they discovered that a few of the local villagers were actually waiting for them! God had also given them a vision that five people from Rajasthan would be visiting them. These simple people did not have any idea where Rajasthan was, but trusted that God's word to them was true.

Thomas Mathews and his team stayed with the local believers and preached the gospel all throughout that region. Many people were healed, delivered from demonic oppression, born-again and ultimately took water baptism under his ministry.

In 1980, Pastor Thomas felt the Lord speak to him out of Revelation 3:8, "Behold, I have set before you an open door, which no one is able to shut." This passage would become a major source of encouragement and promise for Thomas Mathews and his partners. God blessed this small team and through their "faith mission," dozens of local churches were planted in Rajasthan, Gujarat, and Maharashtra. By the end of 1981, over 500 people in that region had been water baptized. During this time, Pastor Thomas Mathews founded the Native Missionary Movement (NMM).[73]

CONTEXT

Dr. Thomas Mathews held firmly to several key principles that would later form the foundation for the growth and expansion of the NMM. These principles or methods encapsulate the ministry philosophy of the Native Missionary Movement.

Incarnational Mission

M.K. Chacko, a mentor and friend to Thomas, advised him to completely lay aside his South Indian identity. He said, "Leave rice and Malayalam, adopt the chappati and Hindi instead."[74] The idea of "mission by immersion" is a core principle

---
73   3 Cherian: 2005.
74   "Dr. Thomas Mathews and His Contribution to Indian Mission". A Souvenir to Commemorate the 50th Year of Pastor Thomas Mathews Coming to Udaipur, sec 03, (2013): 75-77.

and remains a key element to the success of the NMM church planters in North India today.[75]

Progressive Missiology

The willingness to change or adapt the means and methods of mission is an important part of NMM's church planting initiatives. Donald McGavran, the father of the Church Growth Movement was amazed to see that the "people group concept" he was developing was already being utilized in North India missions.

Contextual Mission

Understanding which method and message are the most meaningful for a particular context is a vital component of successful mission strategy in the NMM. Thomas understood the indigenous nature of missions[76] within the broader context of Global mission and worked hard to instill this vision in the church planters and future leaders of the NMM.

Local believers were also encouraged to worship in their own languages, tribal dialects, etc. so as to encourage songwriting and recording in their native tongue.

Native rather than Cross Cultural Missionaries

"Native" missionaries can operate on a much smaller budget, closer to the ones they are serving, and are often more effective and fruitful, since they may enjoy a higher level of acceptance among those who are culturally similar. The focus of discipleship within the NMM came to produce or "re-produce" native, local missionaries from each respective geographical and cultural group. Practically speaking, indigenous believers reaching back into their own communities can make for a more sustainable model of church planting and growth.

---

75 Thomas would sleep, eat, live like those he was ministering to in every way possible. He encouraged all of his church planters to do the same.
76 The methods Mathews used in Rajasthan were different than ones used in Maharashtra.

Church Planting as Mission

The vision of the NMM was to produce "worshipping, caring, and witnessing churches in every village of North India."[77] Evangelism was not seen as an end in and of itself, but rather a means to the larger goal of societal transformation that begins with the community of believers. This emphasis, perhaps explains why there has been such explosive growth among the Filadelfia Fellowship Churches of India (FFCI) churches and believers over the last 50 years.

Self Governing Churches

Churches under the banner of the FFCI enjoy a high level of freedom and function according to their respective cultural and indigenous contexts. Each church is self-governing, self-propagating and self-financing, free from any cultural, administrative, or other demands. Practically speaking, FFCI churches are free to raise funds, train leaders, construct buildings, and use indigenous means in worship.

Theological Education

Thomas Mathews knew the importance of quality theological education. He viewed church planting and theological training as two inseparable aspects of Christian mission, and that quality education produced quality churches. His vision was to produce capable preachers, teachers, church planters, and researchers from within the North Indian mission fields.

Social Mission

Community development quickly emerged as one of the more vital aspects of the NMM. Initially, the focus of Thomas Mathews and the NMM was exclusively on the spiritual transformation of the people through evangelism and church planting. Naturally, there was some discernible social change. The people began to believe God to meet their needs and their change in worldview effected change in their lifestyles, but there was little to no concerted effort in social action at the start. Eventually, all this changed and holistic community development began to emerge as an important aspect of missions. The NMM began to establish

---

77 Lukose: 76.

schools, orphanages, hostels, vocational training institutes, medical clinics, and other community development-focused initiatives.[78]

Resources for Church Growth and Development

Thomas Mathews was a mission leader with a "broad" perspective. As such, he wrote and translated books and other written literature that would contribute to the advance of the gospel. The mission and work has expanded to include many various forms of media.

As a visionary, Dr. Thomas Mathews built, under the leading and guiding of the Holy Spirit, a mission organization that would forever change the face of native missionary efforts in North India.

DEVELOPMENT

Church Planting- Filadelfia Fellowship Church of India (FFCI)

The national level Executive Council for Filadelfia Fellowship Churches of India serves as the governing body of the ministry. Along with the executive council, national and state overseers, area leaders, and local pastors provide the leadership structure for the FFCI. The FFCI is governed by a set of by-laws and is registered with the Indian government. Local pastors are members of the general body and serve as the head of their respective local church committee. Local believers are also involved in serving on the committees in their respective churches.

Approximately 50 years ago, Rajasthan Pentecostal Church (RPC) was founded by Pastor Thomas Mathews upon his arrival in Udaipur. From there, he began to focus on church planting in the surrounding towns and villages. The key ministry strategy was characterized by open air preaching, healing and deliverance, and meeting the felt needs of the local people. Today, miraculous healing, divine deliverance from demons, preaching the word, and empowering the native believers are the most common aspects of church planting by FFCI pastors.

---

78 Pastor Thomas Mathews was often quoted as saying, "We are nation builders". Lukose: 2005. 174. This is an important insight into the emerging holistic vision of the ministry. Building a nation is much more than just church planting. Or perhaps we can say, the church as an instrument of cultural and societal change is able to build a nation?

Filadelfia Fellowship churches have seen steady, albeit moderate, growth over time. Under the oversight of the state council, the area leaders work primarily with the local pastors, church planters, and local believers, providing pastoral care, spiritual oversight and ongoing training.

The Navapur Convention is an annually held conference in Navapur, Maharashtra.[79] The first conference was held in 1981 with a handful of people. Now, there is an average of more than 40,000 people in attendance each year from all over India and the world. This convention is important to the NMM on a local, national, and international level.

Regional conventions also play an important role in the FFCI. These are designed to gather the believers together from all over the region to enjoy a time of fellowship around preaching, worship, and workshops and is a great source of encouragement for the local pastors and believers who also serve as a visible demonstration of the church to local villagers.

Leadership Conferences are held every year at a local level. "Field" pastors and church planters are encouraged to share their experiences with one another, minister to one another through prayer and fellowship, and receive ministry and teaching from FFCI leadership at each of these conferences. These are generally much smaller than the regional and national conferences but are no less critical to the life of the ministry and the continual growth and development of broad-minded, mission-focused ministers.[80] Women's meetings are also held at various times and locations throughout the year. Empowerment through prayer, worship, and theologically sound, practical teaching is a key component to these meetings.

Aravali Region- *Pastor Tajendra Masih, Pai and Pastor Abraham Cherian, Makdadeo*

The Aravali Mountain region located in the southern belt of Rajasthan is home to the Bhils, Meenas, Garasias and various other tribal peoples. Thomas Mathews was encouraged by an experienced priest from the Church of North

---

79 This is the region about which God spoke to Thomas Mathews and his friends about in a vision very early on in his ministry.
80 A "Broadminded" leader refers to the type of leaders that understand the importance of holistic community transformation and are at the forefront of implementation of various community wide development projects. Thus, this is a 'big picture' sort of approach to Kingdom work.

India to begin a work in this area. Pai is a *panchayat*[81] of Udaipur district located in this region. The route from Udaipur city to Pai and Makdadeo was very dangerous due to the activity of *dacoits* or bandits. Many people were afraid to travel this route. However, this did not deter Pastor Thomas Mathews from making his regular trip to this region. Later, after the chief *dracoit* family accepted Jesus as their personal savior, the gospel finally began to penetrate this region.

The mission began when a brother received the baptism of the Holy Spirit through the ministry of Pastor Mathews. This young man was a zealous evangelist and fearlessly shared his newfound faith in Christ with all who would listen. Later, the head *mukhiya* (leader) of the village was water baptized and eventually, the entire family of the chief hereditary Hindu priest of the village came to the Lord as well. The son of this Hindu priest is now an FFCI pastor and has planted four thriving churches in the region.

A short time later, a young Hindu convert who was now a pastor, Tajendra Masih, began to work alongside Thomas Mathews in this region. He adopted a "house church" method of church planting and eventually, established a children's hostel and a small school with the help of World Vision of India.

Today, there are over 40,000 believers in this region. Filadelfia has established over 140 churches, two Bible training centers, four children's homes and three schools to serve this area. In addition, there are three annual region-wide conventions. During these conventions, villagers look to pastors like Tajendra for deliverance from demonic attack, healing, and spiritual guidance. Many people come to Christ as a result of miraculous healing, divine deliverance, and faithful preaching of the Word of God.

Pastor Tajendra exemplifies the core vision of Thomas Mathews in that he is a Bhil pastor, mentored and trained by an "outsider" who then reached back into his own community. As a result, seventy missionaries have been sent out from his

---

81 Panchayat Raj is a system of governance in which gram panchayats are the basic units of administration. It has 3 levels: Gram (village, though it can comprise more than one village), Janpad (block) and Zilla (district). Raj literally means "rule". Mahatma Gandhi advocated Panchayati Raj, a decentralized form of Government where each village is responsible for its own affairs, as the foundation of India's political system. The term for such a vision was Gram Swaraj ("village self-governance"). The leader of the panchayat was generally called the mukhiya, a position which was both hereditary and elected. http://en.wikipedia.org/wiki/Panchayat.

church and he has baptized thousands over the years. The success at Pai has served as a model for other North Indian mission fields.

Pastor Abraham Cherian on the other hand, was raised in a Syrian Christian home in Kerala, India. He was challenged by Pastor Thomas Mathews to go to North India for mission work. After graduating from FBC, he entered the pastoral ministry under Dr. Thomas Mathews. He eventually went on to earn his Ph.D. from Acts Academy of Higher Education, Bangalore, while working in the mission fields of the Aravali Mountains. He has faithfully served the region of Makdadeo for the past 21 years and is now the Regional Overseer of Makdadeo as well as registrar and lecturer at Filadelfia Bible College.

Pastor Cherian is a "foreign" missionary with a Christian upbringing, who learned to *assimilate within* with the people of Makdaeo, much in the same way Pastor Thomas Mathews did. Pastor Tajendra was raised up from *within* his own people, trained and sent back into his own context. Each of these men represent two distinct patterns of mission in the NMM, but share the same (missions) DNA. Tajendra represents rising up *from within* a culture, while Cherian represents the concept of *assimilating into a culture*.

The first FFCI evangelists, church planters, and pastors worked hard to understand and utilize the existing religious worldview of the indigenous tribals as a bridge to begin an open dialogue about Jesus. The prevailing worldview among the people of Aravali is rooted in animism, viewing every sickness, disease, disaster, evil, or calamity, as a direct attack of an evil spirit. Their lives are generally characterized by their efforts to appease these spirits.

The belief in animism helped the villagers identify with "a more powerful spirit," the Holy Spirit, that the Christian missionaries talked about. Through the power of the Holy Spirit, they experienced healing and complete deliverance from demonic oppression and possession. No longer living in fear of the "evil spirits" of their ancestor's faith, they committed themselves to a belief in *Malik*, or the "supreme God" of the Christians.[82]

---

[82] The transition from an animistic worldview to true faith in Christ, is gradual and can be described as a progression in revelation of "Jesus as the healer, exorcist, provider and protector in the context of poor health-care, a spirit worldview, extreme poverty, caste-system and religious persecution". Shaibu Abraham, "Ordinary Indian Pentecostal Christology". (Ph.D. diss., University of Birmingham, 2011). Abstract

Another key factor in the growth and development of the movement is seen in the genuine care for the welfare of women and children demonstrated by the NMM church planters, pastors, and the newly established Christian communities. Until Christian activity started in Makdadeo, women and children had rarely been treated with respect or concern. People who had so often been denied the opportunity to perform the religious functions of their previous religions, now enjoyed the freedom to pray, sing, lead meetings, evangelize, and fellowship with one another. The care and "follow-up" work given to them by the pastors was very well received.

The people also recognized that the Christian pastors spoke with authority to the spirits as they gave "utterance of the remedy" to their situations. This is similar to the functions of the *Bhopa* or village priest, who would come and "chant and give utterances (spells)" on behalf of the afflicted. The early missionaries quickly learned to identify this connection in the mind of the locals and use it as a point of contact with them. Gradually, the real differences or distinctions between these men and the village priest would emerge and the people would begin to pull away from their animistic beliefs and place their trust in Jesus.[83]

In Christ, the locals also find a level of financial freedom. They no longer need to pay for sacrifices, annual and festival related offerings, passing rites, or other related burdens. The missionaries also quickly translated worship songs into the local languages, bringing specific application oriented messages within the new faith.

The churches conduct weekly worship services on Sunday, with Fridays set aside for fasting and prayer meetings. Cottage meetings are regularly held during the week. Special thanksgiving prayers, revival meetings, annual Christmas and New Year fellowship and prayer meetings are also called. These provide much needed time of prayer and fellowship and bond the believing community together.[84]

The neglect the people experienced from the government, and the sense of powerlessness that accompanied it, created a spirit of brokenness among the people. They felt despised and rejected because of their social status. Through their new identity in Christ, the people were empowered by a new sense of hope

---

[83] "A Study Of The Religion Of The Bhils Of Jhadol Taluk In Udaipur, Rajasthan And Their Response To Christian Faith In Post-Independent Period." (M.Th. thesis, Asian Institute of Theology, 2001, 91-92.
[84] Information provided from interview with Dr. Abraham Cherian, the Regional Overseer for Makdadeo.

and acceptance. The Christian ministers and other believers made themselves available to meet the needs of the people and help them in their daily struggles. [85]The establishment of schools, medical clinics, and other community-centered projects, by the people of God, spoke volumes to the locals of the love of Christ for them. The leaders of their former religious systems had demonstrated little or no concern for the practical, social needs of the people and provided nothing by way of community development projects.

The commitment of FFCI churches and its members, can be measured today in terms of their readiness to travel great distances at times for fellowship and prayer meetings. Other believers serve faithfully as itinerant evangelists, traveling regularly over long distances, which keep them away from their families for long periods of time. The level of commitment to the organization and the vision of its founder, Dr. Thomas Mathews, as evidenced by the large (and growing) number of pastors still faithful to the mission, is a good indicator of the level of enthusiasm that is shared by its pastors, church planters, and members.[86]

FFCI pastors are encouraged to receive seminary training whenever possible. As a result, most of the native pastors serving with FFCI have had two or more years of regular seminary training (some training may be through ministry experience and practical level field training). Pastors and leadership conferences, monthly pastors meetings, "First Sunday" fellowships, Christmas fellowship and regional annual conventions provide opportunities for training and fellowship for FFCI pastors and churches.

The understanding of the Word of God and practical level training received from experienced servants of God, have enabled pastors to be influential leaders in their respective communities and make the right decisions in the challenging circumstances that many of them face. In this sense, theological and ministerial training is absolutely necessary for sustainable church planting work and building strong Christian communities. Leadership development and education lies at the heart of the NMM philosophy of mission and is a core value of FFCI churches.

---

85 Information provided from interview with Dr. Abraham Cherian, the Regional Overseer for Makdadeo.
86 In the years 1981-1987, the number of pastors working with Pastor Mathews was 8-10, serving 25 churches. By 2005, the year of his death, there were approximately 800 congregations and around 700 pastors in the FFCI. At present, there are over 1,600 churches and 900 pastors, many of them pastoring multiple congregations. There are usually fifteen to twenty thousand water baptisms annually.

The impact of this movement on other churches or missionary movements has been strong from the beginning. Usually spread by word of mouth, or as our pastors come into contact with leaders from other ministries, the NMM and the FFCI models church planting and community development for many in North India.[87]

Overall, the influence of even a few people in a village can be and often is enough to bring blessing and transformation to the whole community. This transformation usually transcends "community" barriers as well as it spreads throughout the region. What begins with a few people, influences more than a few "people groups," and blossoms into full blown transformational development of the entire region.[88]

The doctrinal (theological) depth of the members of the churches varies from village to village. Most believers, after roughly 15 years of committed faith life and active involvement in the church, are able to give basic theological training to new members.[89] Training, raising up, and sending out "lay" workers empowers the believers, who face many obstacles in their lives, including poverty and discrimination.

New believers often face hatred from their fellow kinsmen and villagers, under the influence of aggressive and intolerant Hindu activists. The attitude of non-Christians toward those who become members of the church is characterized by anger and mistrust.[90]

Consequently, when people and families accept Jesus Christ as their personal Lord and Savior, other family members and neighbors usually respond with shock, contempt, cruelty, and arrogance. Retaliation toward the follower of

---

87 Pastors who have left Filadelfia Fellowship Church of India, for example, generally seem to continue to exhibit the charismatic elements of their Pentecostal heritage in their new ministry context, regardless of the doctrines of their new denominations.
88 The village of Pai, near Makdadeo, in the Aravali Region outside of Udaipur, is under the oversight of Pastor Tajendra Masih. The local *sarpanch* (the elected head of the local self-governing body- *panchayat*) is an active believer in his church. The President of Development Block for the *tehsil*, the Panchayat Samiti, is a believer involved in his church as well. This has contributed greatly to the economic and social development in that region.
89 This assessment is based on a the insight of Pastor Cherian and is indicative of the believers in his charge.
90 Usually, when one starts going to "Yishu's" church, they are seen by the villagers as "one who has denounced the gods and goddesses" associated with their animistic worldview and as one who does not respect the ancestors and the community. They are also seen as a "partaker of the Lord's Supper," which is often referred to as "virgin's urine" by the anti-Christian villagers.

"Yishu" is common practice. The challenge for the believer is to faithfully serve the anti-Christian villagers, so as to meet their various felt needs and perhaps even ultimately help them read and understand the Bible.

In many cases, after seeing that the new believer is standing firm in the faith, people begin to understand their oppositional behavior is foolish and come to respect the faith of the new believer, sometimes even joining them in the faith.

Encouraging new believers to stand firm in the faith, even in the face of persecution and rejection by their family members, and equipping them to do so, will ensure the development of strong, mature believers. This strategy is a key factor in the growth of the influence and longevity of the movement this region.

The number of churches and believers continues to grow gradually. More children receive better quality education than before, and many young people are being trained in the Word of God. Christians increasingly have the potential to transform society on all levels in all walks of life.

Today, many well-financed ministries, both foreign and national, are moving into the harvest fields where NMM church planters have labored for years. These new ministries offer good salaries and other incentives to NMM/FFCI pastors who come and work for them. However, only a relatively small number of pastors have left the NMM for this reason.

The vision is for continued multiplication of churches by having each congregation "beget" one. Each of the existing congregations is asked to adopt an area that has no established church. They then join their faith and resources together to help plant a church and support its growth and development.

FFCI pastors are encouraged to find a "Timothy," in whom he can invest, train, and send, providing practical level training and knowledge, and help support the apprentice minister in his theological education.

Through the schools, children's hostels and various community development projects run by Pastor's Cherian and Tajendra, the NMM is providing affordable, Christ-centered, quality education to everyone in the region as a demonstration of their love for them and for Christ. Graduates can then go on to serve their fellow citizens and country, carrying their influence into all spheres of society.

Filadelfia Bible College

Filadelfia Bible College (FBC) exists to be *"a light to the nations"* by equipping local men and women with knowledge, skill, and passion to revitalize the Church, and fulfill the "Great Commission" in the power of the Holy Spirit. FBC is a ministry of the Native Missionary Movement (NMM), an evangelical Christian institution in the holiness, Pentecostal, and charismatic traditions. The College is committed to the Filadelfia Fellowship Church of India (FFCI), which is itself part of the NMM.

Early on, Pastor Thomas Mathews and his co-workers saw the need for a Bible training center to equip native missionaries to better cope with the challenges they faced in the field. In 1981, five "potential leaders" were selected from among the new believers to be the first students of Filadelfia Bible Institute.

Filadelfia Bible College, as it called today, is a faith venture. In the early stages, classes were conducted in rented homes. Later, God miraculously provided sufficient funds to purchase property near Fatehsagar Lake in Udaipur. A multipurpose "chapel" was constructed and used for classes, student chapel meetings, and church services. This building was dedicated in February 1985. By 1991, the number of students had grown to over 100, making expansion of the facilities necessary. It was also around this time that the name was changed to Filadelfia Bible College (FBC). Students from as far away as Nepal, Bhutan, and Burma began to join the College.

After 30 years, FBC has trained and sent out more than 1,800 students from its Udaipur campus. The programs offered at FBC include Master of Divinity, Bachelor of Theology, Diploma in Theology, and Certificate in Theology, which are taught in English. In addition, a Diploma and a Certificate in Theology are taught in Hindi. In 1992, the Asia Theological Association (ATA) granted accreditation for FBC's degree programs.

The student body at FBC is quite diverse and is representative of the scope and variety of NMM's mission fields. The average age of students is 22 years old, with 37 percent being female and 63 percent male. The student body represents 28 different denominations or denominational affiliations and at least four countries including India, Nepal, Bhutan, and Burma. FBC relies primarily on its network of alumni and pastors in the field to recruit students and does not (usually) advertise outside of internal channels.

In the 2006 – 2007 and again in the 2009 – 2010 academic years, enrollment increased dramatically. This can be attributed to an increased effort on the part of the NMM to encourage field pastors to "identify their Timothy" and send them to the college for proper training. Conversely, a drop in enrollment occurred in the 2002 - 2003 academic year. This drop was due in part to the fact that FBC faculty had not been able to travel as extensively as usual into the NMM mission fields during the previous summer. Thus, there is a direct link between the level and diversity of student enrollment in the college and the level of connection to the mission pastors working with the NMM as an umbrella organization and the FBC as a church body.

There are six regional training centers for local leadership development and training, which also serve as a recruiting center for the FBC.

One of FBC's core values is servant leadership. Faculty and staff seek to lead by example through servanthood (*John 10:11-16, Hebrews 13:17*).

The overall goal of ministerial formation at FBC is to assist in the preparation of men and women for mission and ministry in India, especially North India. The majority of this formation takes place in the classroom through the exploration of scripture and tradition and the thoughtful reflections from a variety of theological traditions.

FBC provides its students with the following:

1. A working knowledge of the history, development, and major themes of the Biblical texts, as well as the historical development of major Christian doctrines (particularly within the Pentecostal tradition), and understanding in contemporary theology. Also important is the development and articulation of a theology of ministry, theology of mission, leadership, pastoral care and homiletics.

2. The capacity to foster ministry related activities: gathering of saints, prayer and worship, teach and transmit the Christian faith to God's people; interpret and preach the Bible in relationship to contemporary life; care and guide believers and their resources with a sense of Christian stewardship; mission related events, evangelism, team leadership, conventions, etc.

3. Commitment to maturity in Christian ministry demonstrated through personal prayer and spiritual counsel, participation in the communal and spiritual life of the Church, Christian dignity and witness, especially in regards to ministerial ethics, continued development of ministerial skills and lifelong learning about the Christian faith, a commitment to the great commission as demonstrated through weekly evangelism, etc.

Field education is an essential component of preparation for mission and ministry. It is designed to move the student beyond the classroom, providing opportunities for the students to realistically test out their vocation within the context of the actual pastoral mission, while developing the habit of theological reflection as an integrative force in combining theoretical knowledge with pastoral experience. Field education for ministry at FBC has three components: experience, supervision, and theological reflection.

Field education should be student-centered and based on an experiential educational methodology. It acknowledges that each person brings to the learning process his or her own particular history and set of experiences. It should also be an educational partnership, where students, supervisors, laypersons and faculty are all part of a network where teaching and learning are mutual.

FBC faculty members often visit mission fields on the weekend. Interested students are given the opportunity to adopt and make regular visits to a nearby village or town for the purpose of conducting Bible studies, preaching, gaining valuable ministry experience, and perhaps shepherding these people after graduation. Orientation events and theological reflection exercises happen throughout the year, particularly during Mission Awareness week and in the second and third years of study.

Spiritual growth is encouraged by promoting the following practices: a disciplined life of prayer and devotional habits (including student led devotions, personal quiet time, and community chapels), a community spirit of worship and support through chapel services and local congregational ministry, and deep mutual accountability with a faculty mentor.

The mentoring program has the following objectives: to strengthen interpersonal relationships, to deepen one's commitment to Christian calling, to provide a safe environment for counseling and meeting other spiritual needs, to expose students to the situations they may face on the Indian mission field, to encourage students to confirm their calling, purpose in life and ministry, receive, develop and/ or articulate their vision, and to prepare them for the future, and all that God has for them.[91]

Mentor groups are another important means of fostering the spiritual development of the students. Staff and students meet informally in designated groups. Filadelfia mentors also meet individually with their students on a regular basis for prayer, counseling, sharing, or simple conversation.

Two or three days are designated as Spiritual Renewal Days each semester. During this time, classes are cancelled and the staff and students join together in fasting and prayer.[92] Additionally, at the end of the second semester, several days are designated as Mission Awareness Days. As the name suggests, these days are filled with mission-oriented teachings and programs designed to instill a passion for mission into the student's hearts, while challenging them to get involved in practical mission activities.

Mentors and faculty gauge the spiritual growth and development of each student by observing students in their punctuality and attendance, self-motivation, willingness to "go the extra mile," ownership of their actions and studies, love and care for younger students, stewardship, interpersonal relationships, and overall willingness to utilize the resources available to them for spiritual growth and development. This includes the student roles in leading prayer, singing, preaching, and serving the community. Some courses are directly related to the practice and implementation of spiritual disciplines.[93]

FBC also receives formal and informal feedback from the mission fields, particularly from Pastors and Regional Coordinators of Filadelfia Fellowship Church.[94] Field pastors also give valuable information regarding the students

---

91 Objectives are taken from FBC internal documents describing the mentoring program.
92 The Spiritual Renewal Day presently coincides, in the first semester, when the team from Durham, England comes to minister. This team has been arriving annually for more than 12 years and always with the focus of spiritual renewal.
93 Keeping the foundational objective of spiritual formation and leadership development in mind, courses such as Spiritual Formation, Discipleship, Life and Work of a Christian Minister, Worship, and Pastoral Care and Counseling, are designed to advance spiritual formation and leadership development. As such, they are core courses in the curriculum.
94 Such feedback helps the college enrich its academic and ministerial formation. In this regard, the relationship between the academic and practical ministry components of the

who visit them on the weekends. These "real-life" settings give students invaluable experience and provide an excellent opportunity for insightful evaluation.

Students are also asked to reflect on their own ministry experiences. At various times in the academic year, individual students or ministry teams share some of their experiences from the field. This takes place either in a chapel setting or during a Fasting and Prayer Day with the school community as a whole.

Pragati Marg Foundation

The Pragati Marg Foundation (PMF) is a limited liability, charitable company registered in June 2011. *The vision is simple: "to go and prepare a world without poverty, by enabling the poor to achieve a sustainable improvement in quality of life through the promotion of economic, social and spiritual development."*

The community related development projects of the PMF, seek to holistically develop communities, starting with the church, and helping individuals to lift themselves out of the cycle of poverty.

Over time, it became clear that even in the regions where the churches had experienced phenomenal growth, issues like poverty, illiteracy, malnutrition, high-cost credit services (annual interest rates ranging from 60-120%), negligible infrastructure, large families, under utilized barren land, lack of irrigation, and cyclical extreme hot, dry weather, still take a devastating toll on the people.[95]

As the name suggests, the PMF creates a path for people to "walk the route to progress on their own." The goal is to help people "visualize a dream, work hard to achieve it, persevering in the process."[96] Through skill development and our various micro-finance initiatives, we are seeing this dream become a reality.

Pragati Marg provides training in business skills, profitable farming, livestock rearing, and health and hygiene. Joint Liability Groups (JLG) and Cluster Liability Groups (CLG) respectively are formed within each local community, providing microcredit for farming, livestock rearing, enterprise start-ups, housing

---

training methodology in the NMM and FBC are essential to leadership development and community transformation.
95 Debidutta Patna, "A Pool In The Whirl Of Issues". A Souvenir to Commemorate the 50th Year of Pastor Thomas Mathews Coming to Udaipur, sec 04, (2013): 92-93.
96 Pattnaik: 93.

development and higher education.[97] As the economic impact of such initiatives is felt within the faith community, the believers are not only able to support themselves financially but also their pastors. The pastor no longer has to carry the burden of both ministry and secular work.

The Pragati Marg Foundation runs a tailoring center named the Jeevan Jyoti Tailoring Center (JJTC). *Jeevan Jyoti* is Hindi for "light of life," which encapsulates the overall vision: providing the light of life through tailoring skills. In line with the United Nation's millennium development plan for the empowerment of women, tailoring is an excellent skill to raise the economic standard of women living in poverty, in a relatively short period of time.

Women living in poverty from the "weaker section of society," suffer hardship in almost every area of life. The PMF is convinced that the empowerment of women living in such conditions, with tailoring skills, is an effective strategy for combating these social issues. There is substantial potential to elevate this neglected sphere of Indian society through the impartation of tailoring skills and/or entrepreneurship opportunities.

The pilot program for the JJTC was initiated in the heart of Kachibasti, the largest slum in Udaipur, located approximately two kilometers from the PMF head office. Our goal is to reach each of the 600 families that reside there.

The Center is established on three core values: focus on the most vulnerable in society, such as the widowed and the abused, focus on women empowerment through providing training skills and thereby giving women in poverty an earning opportunity, and a focus on creating employment. After successful completion of the course upon the recommendation of the instructors, students are enrolled in various internship projects. Interns get the opportunity to earn income, by making and selling bags, women's clothes, etc., while further developing their skills. Select students may also be hired as regular members of the training staff as well.

Laxmi Bai of Nislafala village in Pai, is a handicapped lady born to an extremely poor tribal family. She was affected by polio at a very tender age and lost her ability to walk normally. With the help of her supporting parents, Laxmi completed high school. Unfortunately, her education isn't sufficient enough to earn

---

97 Thristy-two specific case studies will be looked at in the next section.

her a decent job with a good salary. She lives with her parents, without hope of getting married and having her own family.

Laxmi also acquired tailoring skills, but due to the lack of financial resources, she was unable to make use of her skill to support her livelihood. Not long ago, Laxmi was introduced to *Pragati Marg* and helped form a JLG in her area. She financed a loan of Rs. 5000 from the PMF to purchase a motorized-tailoring machine to pursue her tailoring work. Though Laxmi is brushing up on her skills a little bit now, she is not only able to make clothes for her family, but also for the people in her village. In a recent interview, she testified to making up to Rs.100 - Rs.150 every day with her tailoring skills and working machine.

A woman who for a long time considered herself as a burden to her parents is now supporting them, with the support of the PMF. The cluster group is growing quickly and now boasts 15 members. Laxmi serves as the center leader for Nislafala JLG 1 and was recently nominated as the President of the cluster group.

We aim to organize skill-building workshops at CLG levels. The women and CLG members who would not otherwise have access to skills will be given training in weaving, stitching, pickle making, water-filter making, candle making, soap making, small scale engineering, etc.

Education is a foundational means of development in any society. However, in the poor, rural Indian context, there are some practical challenges that call for special attention. The link between illiteracy and poverty cannot be ignored. A recent study reveals that the population below the poverty line for urban Rajasthan is 15.28% and the figure is much larger in rural areas.[98] Many children from poor households are forced into labor at a very early age, hindering their ability to attend school regularly. Their income contributes to the increasing operating cost of running the family, but forces them into a life of hard labor and illiteracy.

According to the 2011 Census, the total population of Rajasthan is 68.6 million, out of which only 67.06% (39 million people) are literate. This is substantially below the national average of 74.04%. The literacy rate for men was

---

98 Population and decadal change by residence: 2011 (PERSONS). Director of Census Operations Rajasthan. http://www.rajcensus.gov.in/PCA_2011_FINAL_DATA/PCA_chapter_1.pdf (accessed April 3, 2014)

80.51%, and for women it was much lower at 52.66%.[99] The local government is trying to improve literacy at the primary level in many villages; it is struggling to find an adequate number of qualified staff. The highest gross enrollment rate of students in villages is 52%. In some villages, the ratio of teachers to classes is 3:1 or worse. As a result, schools are unwilling to enroll new students, making the enrollment rate even lower. Additionally, teacher absenteeism is on the rise. In one survey it was found that 60% of the children aged 6-12 could not read a simple paragraph in English.

Another obstacle is private institutions that do not see running a school in the village as an economically viable option for them and by and large, are not interested in rural/village education initiatives. In some of the few places that adequate schools have been established, the fee structure is usually beyond the capacity of a poor villager. Hence, students in rural areas receive inferior education and as a result, find it difficult to compete for jobs in the city.

PMF aims to address some of the above-mentioned issues by implementing the following strategies. First, our poverty eradication programs develop the economy of the poor, thereby reducing the burden on the children in the family. Second, parents are counseled or encouraged to send their children to school. Third, as an organization committed to social action, we bring awareness about various government-run scholarship programs; helping merit-list students from poor families obtain scholarships to meet their expenses. Finally, we raise funds to support poorer local schools by contributing towards staff salary, course development, and motivating them to continue offering services for the poor children.

Because of its rich cultural heritage, beautiful locations, palaces, and historical monuments, Rajasthan is able to attract tourists from all over the world. Tourism has emerged as a major industry for most regions of Rajasthan. Many villagers, however, fail to take advantage of this due to a lack of communication skills in English. As a special focus to improve the employment opportunities of villagers, we are planning in the near future to initiate small spoken English and computer literacy coaching centers.

---

99   Population and decadal change by residence: 2011 (PERSONS). Director of Census Operations   Rajasthan.http://www.rajcensus.gov.in/PCA_2011_FINAL_DATA/PCA_chapter_3.pdf (accessed April 3, 2014)

We also aim to help the community of believers and the poor achieve economic sustainability through access to financial services. Primary source banks are reluctant to lend to the rural poor, due to the lack of collateral, high risks, and high costs of loaning to poorer clients, or in some cases the lack of branches in remote areas. As a result, many villagers do not have access to financial services and are, therefore, left in the hands of moneylenders. These lenders exploit the poor by charging up to 60% interest per annum. Poverty caused by unemployment and underemployment is also a long-standing issue for the rural population of Rajasthan. Thus, provision of standard financial services, strengthening the most basic economic activity of the poor (i.e. agriculture, farming, live-stock rearing, micro-enterprises, etc.) is crucial to their survival.

The concept of micro-finance is to provide small-scale loans to people who do not have access to bank loans. This is achieved by operating low-cost branch offices, organizing clients into clusters, or in some cases joint-liability groups, who take responsibility for each other. The field officers undertake regular cluster group meetings and monitoring activities. This model of lending has had considerable success worldwide, and has been shown to have a major impact on the lives of the poor.[100] The micro-loan portfolio of the PMF consists of Agricultural, Business, Housing, and Education Loans. Agricultural and Business Loans comprise more than 75% of the portfolio.

Agricultural Loans are given to individual poor farmers, in joint liability groups, for a maximum term of 12 months. These loans are typically given for the purpose of growing cash crops such as muesli, ginger, ratalu (purple yam), and turmeric. Farmers use a small portion of their land to grow the cash crops alongside their usual staple crops. A single loan of 10,000 rupees (Indian Rupee- INR) or approximately $165 US Dollars (USD), given for growing muesli can yield a profit of four to five times that amount during the harvest.[101] The PMF provides the farmers with water pumps that enable them to preserve the crop within the ground and harvest them only when demand is high, and hence bring a good price for their crops. The average return of such crops after provisions for seed, fertilizer,

---

100 Debidutta, Pattniak. "A Pool In The Whirl Of Issues". A Souvenir to Commemorate the 50th Year of Pastor Thomas Mathews Coming to Udaipur, sec 04, (2013): 93.
101 A survey conducted by PMF reveals that during the first few months of the harvesting season, the price plummets due to an excess supply of Musli. The best price of about Rs. 50,000 ($825 USD) is achievable usually after 3-4 months into harvesting when the excess supply is not driving the prices down.

insecticides, labor fees of Rs. 12,000 ($198 USD), and loan repayment is good. The overall profitability of this venture is around 32%. Thus, ideally, it takes a few loan cycles to make the farmer self-sustainable.

Sardara Bhai is a resident of Manas Village, approximately 33 miles away from Udaipur, who was living in impoverished conditions. In April 2010, Sardara Bhai was introduced to the PMF. At this point, the PMF was still in its infancy. We discovered that this man has some land in an area that could potentially foster growth of cash crops (e.g. muesli- a medicinal herb) along with the usual staples of corn, maize, etc. Along with a few other friends from the region, Sardara Bhai was enrolled into the farming development pilot project scheme *Krishivikas*.[102] He was given 10 kilos of muesli seed worth Rs.6000 ($90 USD) including interest. The project started in the month of June 2010. Sandra and his wife were faithful in following the directions and objectives of the scheme.

By November 2010, their muesli harvest was tested and discovered to be the best in quality for the entire region. Sardara Bhai sold his muesli and received Rs. 24,000 ($400 USD) in less than 7 months time, preserving about 30 kilos for next season. He repaid the entire loan amount, and immediately took out another loan for Rs.10,000 ($165 USD) to enroll his daughter into a Bachelor's of Education program. At the end of the second farming cycle, in January 2012, Sardara Bhai sold 100 kilos of muesli, earning him Rs. 120,000 ($1,900 USD) and had sown more than 50 kilos for the third farming cycle in June 2012. A family, who were almost hopeless in June 2010, with the little bit of support from the PMF, is witnessing their treasured dreams come true in life. Now, Sardara's daughter is qualified as a teacher, earning the same amount her father struggled his entire life to earn.

There are many families in poverty with highly unproductive land, who mostly depend on irregular manual labor available in the city. So, self-employment is proving to be a useful strategy for improving the income levels of such households currently in poverty. Business Loans are given to individuals in joint liability groups either to start a small business or to expand an existing one. The loan term is for a maximum period of 18 months. In our business loans, clients are offered loans to run small-scale businesses such as grocery stores, milk centers, poultry shops, vegetable shops, and hardware stores.

---

102   Krishi means "agriculture" and vikas means "development" in Hindi.

With a loan of roughly Rs. 5000 ($82 USD) and a little training in small business management, raising and selling live chickens can be a highly profitable venture. The poor can achieve a useful source of livelihood in one year's time. The fixed cost expenses for things like a cage, weighing scale, etc. are managed within Rs. 1000 ($16 USD). The rest of the loan amount is used for purchasing birds and feed. Basically, birds of lighter weight are purchased at a lower price, grown to a good weight and then sold to the customers for a profit. The average purchase price per bird is Rs. 80 ($1.30 USD); approximately 45 birds can be purchased and later sold at Rs. 130 ($2.15). The business unit can achieve a gross profit of 63% on each bird, which can be reinvested to make a livelihood.

Before his introduction to the PMF, Shantilal was an evangelist and the pastor of a local congregation of about 30 poor families. Most of the converts in Palawada, a village near Makadadeo, earn their livelihood as seasonal laborers, farming, etc. They are poor and unable to support the pastor financially. Shantilal would also hire himself out as a laborer for income before joining the PMF. With the support of Shantilal and few other families of Palawada, the PMF started a cluster group there and he served as the president. After few months, he approached the PMF to help him start a small business. He was given training and a loan of Rs. 10,000 to start a small mobile trolley business, selling vegetables, eggs, biscuits, and other edibles. He earns approximately Rs. 200-250 per day. His business is growing at the moment, meeting the daily needs of his family of five.

Housing loans are given to individuals who regularly attend cluster group meetings upon the recommendations of the other cluster group members. The loan term is a maximum period of 60 months. With progressive growth in income levels of the poor, improved living conditions become the next immediate need. Our housing loan is devised to cater to such needs. In a housing loan, we dispense longer-term loans for construction, repair, or modification of houses. The repayments are made from the regular cash flow of the household.

Education is undoubtedly one the foundational means for development in any society. The PMF desires to facilitate services for enabling children from poor households to be professionally educated in some trade. Education loans are given to individuals who regularly attend cluster group meetings and with the recommendations of the other cluster group members. The PMF educational loans have a maximum term of 24 months. The repayments are made from the regular cash flow of the household.

Practices

Filadelfia Fellowship Churches of India (FFCI) was formed in 1987 out of the growing need to account for the scope and depth of the work, and as a resource for the ever-growing number of village pastors, evangelists, and church planters. During his lifetime, Thomas Mathews saw around 1,200 churches planted in thirteen different North Indian states during his 42 years of ministry. This is an average of 2-3 new church plants per month! As of this writing, over 1,600 FFCI churches have been established, serving about 300,000 believers throughout north India.

Shortly after the founding of the NMM, the need arose to establish a Spirit-filled Bible training center to help the leaders of the NMM develop and pass on a sound spiritual and theological Christian witness. The focus of this would be to: equip native missionaries to cope with the new challenge of church planting, growth, and multiplication. Five potential leaders were selected from among the believers to be the first students of Filadelfia Bible Institute (FBI). Filadelfia Bible College was established in 1982 as the main training and equipping arm of the Native Missionary Movement and has since sent out 1,800 graduates into North Indian mission fields.

St. Mathews Senior Secondary School was founded in 1998 on the conviction that education is one of the most powerful vehicles of societal change. The first school was established in Kotra, followed by Udaipur, which has the largest school with over 1,000 students. These schools[103] are taught in English and provide affordable, quality education to over 3,000 children from all segments of society.

Pastor Mathews used to preach a "holistic" approach to outreach. That is, the believer is called to "care about the spirit, soul, and body of a person." In the year 2000, a team of 12 doctors came to conduct medical camps in several villages. This gave rise to the vision for a more "permanent" solution to the health care problems of the people in that region. Today, Grace Hospital, founded in 2011, is a fully equipped, 70 bed Christian Mission Hospital, serving the needs of the

---

103   There are seven schools located in Pai, Saira, Jhadol, Makdadeo, Gogunda, Navapur, and Udaipur.

local tribal people in Navapur, Maharashtra. Local NMM churches annually host medical camps and health clinics to impact the community with the love of Christ.

The NMM's publishing initiatives are envisioned to empower people through Spirit-inspired Christian resources. By creating diverse Christian resources through print, audio, and visual mediums, our desire is to enable every person and church to grow into the fullness of Christ. To this day, there is little Christian literature available in Hindi. Cross and Crown Publishing was established in 1971 to address this growing need. Today, the vision of Cross and Crown remains under the name of Open Door Publications Private Limited (ODP). The vision for media is to develop a media ministry that will not only act as a pioneer, but also be a high quality, integrated hub for all media solutions to reach the lost for Christ. Translation of theological materials into Hindi remains a major part of the media ministry of the NMM.[104] Currently Open Door is involved in publishing Hindi worship CD's,[105] audio CD's, and is working on an updated Hindi Bible.[106]

Realizing the vision for the holistic development of the church, the Pragati Marg Foundation, founded in 2010, is taking issues such as poverty, illiteracy, malnutrition, negligible infrastructure, high cost credit services, and lack of irrigation facilities, head on. Building on the foundation laid over 50 years ago, the PMF serves as the "face" of a preexisting ministry philosophy, stressing the development of the whole person and community in which the church exists. The Pragati Marg Foundation is active in micro-finance, animal husbandry, sustainable/profitable farming, vocational skill development, health and hygiene education, and housing and business development. So far, over 600 families have benefitted from the impact of the PMF initiatives.

LEARNINGS

The vision of the NMM is to reach India with the love of Christ. Pastors and missionaries provide the needed leadership to realize that vision. They establish faith communities, build up believers spiritually, economically, and socially, and teach them to engage their communities on all levels.

---

104 Many books have been translated, written, printed and distributed across North India by NMM.
105 To date, approximately fifteen Christian worship resources have been recorded on CD.
106 Over one hundred thousand gospel tracts have been printed by Cross and Crown (Open Door) and distributed by NMM pastors and evangelists.

Church planting has been the first step in community transformation. Everywhere that the NMM church planters and missionaries have gone, a faith community is established. The primary method is prayer, accompanied by signs and wonders. Following the feeding of the soul comes the nourishment of the mind and body through various social and educational initiatives. Producing strong leaders requires an adequate means of education. Schools like St. Matthews are a double-edged sword in this regard.

Signs and wonders remain a key component in the establishment of the church/faith community. However, other avenues of outreach are opening up in the form of schools, hospitals, medical clinics, children's hostels, etc. Deliverance from demonic oppression, miraculous healing, and confrontations with evil spirits are necessary for complete deliverance once a person decides to join the faith community, but it may have been the new school placed in the region by the NMM that first peaked their interest in the Christians. The two work hand in hand.

Reliance on the Holy Spirit to guide the work is essential. Spirit-filled pastors and church planters are sensitive to the leading and guiding of the Holy Spirit. This is true whether they are teaching the believing community or strategically engaging in community development projects. There is a two-fold focus on the Holy Spirit and the Word in every NMM project. For Thomas Mathews, church planting through evangelism and the miraculous was the primary impetus of individual and community wide change. More ministries developed as various needs emerged.

Pastors have been and continue to rely on God for provision, and believers are eager to give. Equally real however, are the issues of poverty and illiteracy that plague most villages in India. God moves mightily in healing and signs and wonders, but he is also moving through the efforts to fight the social ills of the culture at the grassroots level. Confronting the enemy on both levels is the primary task of the Christian community. Working to empower the church is the first step.

Much success can be attributed to the strategic contextualization of worship, church meetings, community fellowship, and strategic community development projects. NMM church planters adapt to the environment they're working in, thus enabling them to contextualize the gospel appropriately based on the local cultural dynamics.

Micro-finance programs are also tailored appropriately based on the needs of the people. If the greatest need is education, a school can be built. If the greatest need is clean water, a well will be dug. Contextualizing the means of communication of the gospel, in partnership with the Word and the Holy Spirit is key to the establishment of the faith community and its sustainability. (In other words, all elements are needed but were not always present in the early days. They are all present today, but not necessarily in the same order.)

Human development is realized in spiritual transformation and in meeting felt needs. This realization gave rise to the establishment of the Pragati Marg Foundation, Grace Hospital, and various other needs-based ministries. Thomas Mathews was always involved in meeting people's needs, but formal ministry initiatives developed gradually over time. Empowerment of women, skill development, animal husbandry, tailoring, and agricultural schemes were formed with human development in mind, beginning with the believers.

The faith community should become a transformative community. On this level the believers are experiencing the reality of transformation in their own lives. Pragati Marg plays an important role in moving the faith community into a transformative community by offering socio-economic opportunities not otherwise available to them. Once the social or educational standard of the believing community has been elevated and others take notice of it, the believers are able to speak into their lives and offer them the same hope they have. Signs, wonders, and miracles still play an important role, but are now complimented by the social aspect of the gospel. The transformation that has taken place in the believers lives is now on display.

The transformative community then becomes a reaching community as the focus becomes outward. Social projects, community development, health care, and meeting the felt needs of the surrounding community come into focus. Good education produces good pastors, which produces good churches, which produces good citizens, which are needed for transformation to be made at any level.

Dedicated leaders are the backbone to the ministry. Leaders, who focus on the big picture of expansion and multiplication, reproduce other like-minded leaders, thus producing a steady flow of leadership within the movement.[107] Faith

---

107 Abraham Cherian in Makdadeo region is an example of this. Pastor Thomas Mathews challenged him to come to North India, imparted vision, trained, raised him up, and sent

communities led by dedicated leaders who's DNA is mission are the future of the ministry. This reality points to the important role education plays in leadership development. Leadership development in this context includes both secular and theological training. The importance of good theological training in leading the church cannot be overstated. The challenge, however, is equipping young men and women from the village context in theology who may be illiterate or have a very low level of education. This points to the need for the establishment of primary and secondary schools as an extension of the broader "kingdom agenda" of transformational development.[108]

When a student receives a solid foundation of education at a young age, they are more inclined to see the value of education and there is a greater chance of them contributing to society in a positive way. Through education, their socio-economic situation can change, enabling future generations to reap the benefits. The church and Indian society as a whole, has and will continue to benefit from education.

Founding the ministry with a flexible missiology is what really laid the foundation for these ministries. Purposeful, strategic planning of community development initiatives, in partnership with the work of the Holy Spirit in signs and wonders, has emerged as the key. Additionally, the health of the believing community is measured by its mission zeal. Mission-driven communities are transformational communities, ones that produce tangible change on multiple levels of society. Self-replicating, missional, transformational communities are the goal and have been the pattern across the mission fields.

FUTURE

Spiritual transformation through salvation in Christ naturally brings about a level of social transformation in a person's life. Freedom from demonic oppression, a miraculous healing, or poverty eradication are all means to the end of community transformation. A person may come to Christ as a result of miraculous healing, but discipleship by a strong, qualified leader must follow. Thus, emphasizing the importance of theological education and leadership development from FBC, and

---

him out. Now Pastor Cherian is doing the same with young men and women in Makdadeo and FBC.
108 FBC has the goal of seeing at least ten North Indians students come through the college, work towards their PH.D.'s, and ultimately contribute to global theological dialogue.

spiritual transformation needs to continue to be emphasized alongside of societal transformation in future endeavors.

The sustainability of the movement depends in large part on the quality of leaders it produces. But this is not done in a vacuum. It takes a holistic approach to human development to produce quality leaders. The reality of illiteracy and substandard education in the villages presents a formidable challenge to proper theological education, thus emphasizing the need for more schools in the villages raising the overall standard of education. It is critical that educational projects continue in the future, if we hope to produce quality Christian leaders within the local context.

Students who come to FBC with a good education already in place, generally excel in their studies, becoming leaders who can effect change in multiple spheres of society. Typically, the planting of a church follows the founding of a school in a region, although this is not always the case. Educational initiatives, which work to develop the community as a whole and enforce the church planting work, go hand-in-hand with the overall goal of leadership development. In this way, the work of the NMM is cyclical in operation but linear in movement towards its goal. This dynamic of education and church planting, leading to spiritual and societal transformation, resulting in trained quality Christian leaders who can then go out and plant more churches and build more schools is a healthy, successful cycle for a strong local church in India.

The DNA of the faith communities is reaching out to others. This is the means by which replication and revitalization take place. With this understanding, church-planting ministry can be defined in a variety of ways. It can be starting a school, or opening a tailoring training center. It can also mean implementing a strategic community development program through micro-finance loans. Church planting in this context is synonymous with community transformation, starting with the community of believers and reaching out to all.

Case Report and Analysis

There are several clearly identifiable factors that have contributed to the success of this ministry to date:

By far, the most obvious and perhaps crucial factor is the "DNA of missions" that characterized the life and ministry of the founding father, Dr. Thomas Mathews. His vision, commitment, and integrity, influenced in part by the Lausanne Movement, Donald McGavern, and the writings of John Wesley was contagious and played a key role in the expansion of the ministry. He was a very charismatic leader who was able to draw many young people to himself.

Through his leadership and the significant role of the Holy Spirit, many young pastors and leaders were developed and placed in ministry under FFCI, many of who remain today. The "DNA of missions" was implanted deeply into the hearts and minds of all those who Thomas and Mary Mathews encountered in those early days. They were very incarnational in their ministry approach, choosing to live among those whom they were ministering to. This facilitated the transfer of DNA to take place and strengthened the bonds between minister and believer, laying the groundwork for sustaining the movement. One could characterize this mission theme as: "train a Timothy and adopt an outstation." Raise up. Send out.

Key contributing factors to revitilization

Water baptism is given only to those who are ready to take the challenges associated with it and as such, has emerged as an identifying mark of a Christ follower within one's tribal or village context and within the Christian community as a whole.

Contextualization of the gospel message is a key to the revitalization of the movement. It was important to the founding of the ministry and remains equally if not more so today. As such, each local church is given the freedom to worship in their own language and in their own way.

The freedom from addiction to alcohol is also characteristic of the change that accompanies transformation. This happens after a community has been touched by the Holy Spirit through the work of an FBC student or FFCI minister or evangelist.

Significance of leadership model

Thomas Mathews was a God-appointed, Holy-Spirit-led apostle to India who influenced many with his life and ministry. Simply put, we need more men like him!

Grass roots level evangelism/ministry

"Power evangelism" at the grassroots level is a key contribution to the continued growth and revitalization of the movement. That is, our methodology is evangelism accompanied by signs, wonders, healings, and exorcisms. This is the most effective way of reaching the unreached segments of Indian society at the most basic fundamental level of felt needs.

Church growth

Sustainable church growth and expansion is the goal. In the first 18 years of existence, the number of FFCI churches went from 25 to 800 churches or congregations and 700 pastors. In 2005, the number had increased to 1600 churches and 900 pastors with some pastors leading multiple churches. Many of these churches are led by FBC graduates.

Missions: methods, challenges and opportunities

Church Ministry

There is still a strong need for qualified leadership at the local congregational level. Raising up strong, charismatic leaders to fill this void remains a priority for FFCI and FBC. The believers must be given adequate training in the word in order for the gospel to spread and have maximum impact in the culture.

School Ministry: "Plundering the Egyptians"

Having teachers from different religions and social standings presents a unique set of challenges and opportunities. Caste concerns and internal challenges from the staff and faculty can also contribute to any challenges in the area of education.

We've adopted a strategic approach to accommodate the strengthening of the church. Many of the believers' children attend the school at a free or reduced rate. This is made possible by the fees of the other students who can afford to pay full price for their tuition. This allows the school to cover its operating costs while providing CBSE board-certified, quality education to the children of the region, particularly the Christian community. This form of empowerment for the believing community is very effective.

Community Development

Pragati Marg Foundation

The goal of obtaining economic transformation through micro-finance is designed first, with the believer in mind. When a believer or believing community is supported economically they are able to give back to the church, thereby blessing the pastor and his family and eventually all of those around them. In this way, there is spiritual blessing and relief from material poverty.

One challenge is in teaching accountability and responsibility to the recipients of the loans. Local cluster groups are in place to help in this regard but some challenges still remain.

Opportunities

Financial resources are often times at a minimum. This makes it difficult to pay the pastors in the field in a timely fashion or with regularity. This can lead to unnecessary tension and interfere with the work.

It is also difficult for the local or national leadership to visit all of the mission fields regularly, especially as the ministry expands. Thus there is a continual emphasis on raising up leaders for these churches and mission stations.

Leadership Development

Most of the top leaders of NMM are south Indian Malayalees from Kerela. The desire is to see more local, north Indian leadership raised up in the future. The faculty at FBC is fairly multi-ethnic but more work remains in this area. The mission fields are in north India. Leadership for these areas should come from north India. We continue to work towards this end. There has been at times the appearance of nepotism among the leadership.

Identifying Leaders

The faculty at FBC try to identify those students who display leadership qualities and giftings. These students are encouraged to develop in their gifting and are groomed for leadership. Those students who display academic prowess are encouraged to pursue higher studies and are sponsored by the college to do so.[109]

Infrastructures

The increased size of the ministry has made it difficult to remain focused only in building people, with the expansion of ministry we need to build structures. Our vision is for statewide regional centers to facilitate all five ministries.

Emerging Biblical/Theological Concepts

Prayer is a significant element of the movement. As a result, fasting and prayer is a regular practice in the churches. Students engage monthly in all night intercessory prayers and believers are taught to pray.

The power of God is manifest and testified to, not only by the pastors or evangelists, but by all the believers. Powerful and effective prayers resulting in miracles and signs and wonders are commonplace. Pastors and students are living the Book of Acts as a reality. Their is a strong reliance on the move/power of the Holy Spirit in each local church.

Dependence on God for all provision is a characteristic of our leadership. Leaders exercise faith in all areas of their lives and teach their believers how to do the same. This is evidenced by the role of lay leadership in prayer, giving/hearing testimonies, and in motivating, educating, and instructing the people about God's work in their lives.

Thomas Mathew was careful not to bring the Malayalee culture to North Indian culture. Additionally, he worked with Christians from other traditions, instructing them to be filed with the spirit and power. Pentecostal "fire" was brought to the mission field through his work.

---

109 One Bhil is pursuing a PhD from ACTS.

Initially, Thomas Mathews was also against the wearing of ornaments after conversion. Eventually, with the growth of the church, he only spoke against the wearing or retention of religious ornaments or icons.

A progressive Christology emerged over time, moving believers from a Pneumatological understanding/experience to a solid biblical Christology, recognising Jesus as their savior.[110] This resulted from the strong emphasis on the preaching of the Word of God in the meetings.

Living exemplary lives of integrity and the demonstration or practical instruction of ministry is characteristic of NMM leadership. Striving to give the "best to the least" has emerged as a significant theme among the leadership of NMM.

How can we expand the biblical/theological understanding?

Personal experience of God's work in the context of ministry is significant. The word of God is active and alive, bringing revelation. The presence and manifestation of the Holy Spirit is central in the expansion as well.

Expansion is accompanied by transformation of individuals and societies. Empowering is the motive of expansion. Expansion is characterised as a journey of experience.

We move the believers from experience to relationship to knowledge to logic (reasoning). We build from the experience. The question that emerges here is, "Who is Jesus in our churches?". That question is answered best by the following progressive Christology listed below.

Several levels of Christology (Progressive Christology)

1. Healer (sickness)

2. Exorcist (demons)

3. Protector (animistic context – good and evil forces, fear of ancestors)

4. Provider (support)

---

110 See below, "Who is Jesus in our Churches?"

5. Savior (salvation - ready for baptism)

6. Lord, supreme God

We must develop/promote a contextual theology – theology of oral songs and music in tribal Christian contexts- that identify the beliefs and balance the understanding to bring true salvation and a relationship with Jesus to the people.

Our conviction is that transformation affects the whole nation. Economic progress emerges out of this transformation. The new believers no longer have to spend money on appeasing the gods and *pujaries*. Development is a real process that takes time and commitment both to the people and the process itself.

It's important to promote a sense of belonging. Celebration as part of the culture is continued in conventions – locally and regionally. Multiple caste groups are brought together – not just in house fellowships, but also in village gatherings and in a monthly, common meal. In this way, the church is seen as a caring community.

Marriage ceremonies and many other customs continue even after conversion. The church is involved in marriage proposals when the proper age is reached. The elderly desire to be dedicated like the children are.

What's next for Filadelfia?

Filadelfia has 300,000 believers, touching only 3,000 families. There is still so much to do, specifically in leadership formation, fundraising, and resource acquisition, development, and distribution.

The vision for the future is to see the current leadership committed to pass on the vision of the founder and "transfer" the DNA of missions to the future leaders. Several initiatives are in place to facilitate this process. Its essential to expand the vision: "train a Timothy and adopt an outstation." This will facilitate continued growth and revitalization of the movement. We desire to plant at least 35 churches every year- having students involved in church planting while pursuing their studies. This is an essential ingredient in producing quality leaders for the church and society. Its also important to take the theology of the institution to the pastors in the field providing further training for ministry and development.

Organizational Structure

Dr. Thomas Mathews oversaw all aspects of the ministry prior to his death in 2005. Mrs. Mary Thomas now provides top leadership with the trust, managing the ministries and providing the overall accountability for the ministry. The local leaders provide the "day-to-day" oversight.

Building our capacity to facilitate the revitalization of the ministry and for reaching our goals is a large component of our future planning. (Currently, we facilitate extension studies for pastors-Union Biblical Seminary, MDiv and William Carey International University, MA in International Development). We continue to bring in and raise up professional teachers to cover the huge geographical span of the ministry as well developing traveling teachers to reach into the various training centers and village contexts.

Additionally, the goal is for every state is to have a regional mission center/station to facilitate all five branches of ministry. (One such center already exists in Rajasthan.)

In 1987, Mrs. Mary Mathews pioneered an effective ministry initiative in MP state. Women took over the leadership role during a season of intense persecution in Jhabua, where 14 FFCI pastors were imprisoned. The role of women in the ministry cannot be overstated in our mission fields.

Directions for practical actions towards Christian revitalization:

Praying for men of God like Thomas Mathews to answer the call for missions is key – God uses individuals with special call and anointing. He was passionate about church planting. May the Lord raise more such leaders of vision and influence. We also pray that many others will catch the vision of NMM. When people come forward in response to God's call, the church at large needs to pray for and support them.

We continue to tell the stories of men and women who have "gone before," suffered, and set an example for us. Retelling a new generation, reminding them of their heritage, will help produce more like-minded, kingdom-focused people, encouraging them to engage in all aspects of the ministry. The content of theological education connects with the reality of people in the context of churches, equipping them for every task.

Revitalization consultation participant reflections

1. This is the Lord's doing and it is amazing in our eyes.

2. The courage of the leaders in taking risks for the tasks at hand.

3. We can clearly see that God gives gifts to His people to do the ministry.

4. It is clear that the ministries are designed to meet the needs of the people.

5. Our ministry motto within the congregation is "Every believer knowing their inheritance in God and moving in power."

6. Church planting is synonymous with community transformation.

7. It is all faith and vision – the seed from the founder is being sown, followed, and built upon.

8. The trinity of mission in NMM is – church planting, education and leadership development, and community development.

Works Cited

Abraham, Shaibu
    2011   "Ordinary Indian Pentecostal Theology." Ph.D. diss., University of Birmingham.

Cherian, Abraham T.
    2001   "A Study of the Religion of the Bhils of Jhadol Taluk in Udaipur, Rajasthan and Their Response to Christian Faith in Post-Independent Period." M.Th. thesis, Asian Institute of Theology.

    2005   "Contribution of Churches and Missions to the Bhils of Rajasthan." Ph.D. diss., Asia Institute of Theology.

    2013   "I will Build my Church," in *A Souvenir to Commemorate the 50th Year of Pastor Thomas Mathews Coming to Udaipur*, section 4:86-86.

Christian, Charles
    2013   "A Light to The Nation: Education as Mission," in *A Souvenir to Commemorate the 50th Year of Pastor Thomas Mathews Coming to Udaipur*, section 4:96-97.

Directorate of Census Operations Rajasthan
    2011   Population Enumerations-2011; Chapter 1: Population, Size and Decadal Change. http://www.rajcensus.gov.in/PE_DATA.html (accessed April 3rd, 2014).

    2011   Population Enumerations-2011; Chapter 3: Literates and Literacy Rate. http://www.rajcensus.gov.in/PE_DATA.html (accessed April 3rd, 2014).

Gavit, Samuel
    2011   "The Ministry of the Word of God in FFCI with Special Reference to Selected Churches at Navapur." Master's thesis, Filadelfia Bible College.

Lukose, Wessley
    2001   "A Contextual Missiology of the Spirit: A Study of Pentecostalism in Rajasthan, India." Ph.D. diss., University of Birmingham.

    2013   "Dr. Thomas Mathews and His Contribution to Indian Mission," in *A Souvenir to Commemorate the 50th Year of Pastor Thomas Mathews Coming to Udaipur*, section 3: 75-77.

    2013   "Filadelfia Bible College and the Missional Explosion in North India," in *A Souvenir to Commemorate the 50th Year of Pastor Thomas Mathews Coming to Udaipur*, section 4: 88-89.

Pant, Rahul
    2013   "His Word Runs Swiftly: Harnessing media to equip and evangelize," in *A Souvenir to Commemorate the 50th Year of Pastor Thomas Mathews Coming to Udaipur*, section 4: 94-95.

Pattnaik, Debidutta
    2013   "A Pool in the Whirl of Issues," in *A Souvenir to Commemorate the 50th Year of Pastor Thomas Mathews Coming to Udaipur*, section 4: 92-93.

Philip, Finny
    2013   "The Thomas Mathews Revolution," in *A Souvenir to Commemorate the 50th Year of Pastor Thomas Mathews Coming to Udaipur*, section 3: 80-82.

Philip, John
    2004   "A Study of Native Missionary Movement with Special Reference to Rajasthan." Master's thesis, Union Biblical Seminary.

P.G., Marykutty
    2006   "A Comparative Study of the Role of Women in Ministry in the Early Church and the Involvement of Women in Native Missionary Movement." B.D. thesis, Union Biblical Seminary.

Punnoose, Chacko
    2008   "Developing a Homogenous Church Planting in India." Ph.D. diss., Evangelical Theological Seminary.

Regimen, K.
    2005 "The Mission Works of Filadelfia Fellowship Church of India among the Bhil Tribe of Banswara District of Rajastan and its Impact." Master's thesis, New Life Bible Seminary.

Samuel, J.
    2006 "A study on the influence of Rajasthan Pentecostal Church in the Socio-Economic Upliftment of the Bhil Tribes in Udaipur District." Master's thesis, Asian Institute of Theology.

Thomas, C.P.
    2011 "The Concept of Power Encounter in Mission of Selected Pentecostal Churches of Rajasthan with Special Reference to the Bhil Tribes." Master's thesis, Union Biblical Seminary.

Titus, Merin
    2013 "Caring for the Spirit, Soul and Body," in *A Souvenir to Commemorate the 50th Year of Pastor Thomas Mathews Coming to Udaipur*, section 4: 90.

Varughese, Regi
    2005 "Miracles and Filadelfia Fellowship Church of India, Banswara District Rajasthan: A Theological Appraisal." B.M. thesis, Filadelfia Bible College.

Concluding Remarks: Consultation in World Christian Revitalization Movements

NEW THEOLOGICAL COLLEGE
DEHRA DUN, INDIA
JAMES C. MILLER

Based on the five case studies and the examination of those studies at the Consultation, this essay seeks 1) to identify and comment upon recurring themes that emerged across the cases, 2) to reflect upon the practice of Christian revitalization as it occurs in this context, and 3) to suggest avenues for the future promotion and sustenance of Christian revitalization.

The thematic similarity of the case studies provides solid ground for comparative analysis. To a significant degree, they concentrate upon institutions devoted to theological education and their faithfulness to their stated missions. Four of the studies examined theological colleges and associated churches launched out of these colleges. The fifth study explored a church planting movement, but one associated with a theological college. Thus, we have ample reason to analyze these cases, looking for emerging themes among them.

Recurring Themes

Three themes reverberated throughout the course of our discussions. The first involved missional integrity. This issue was raised in several ways, often through questions such as, " 'Are we actually accomplishing what we think we are?'", " 'Have we lost our vision?'" or " 'Has our vision changed in some manner?'".

The second concerned the nature and effectiveness of theological education more broadly. This was voiced in the oft-heard concern about the vital connection, or lack thereof, between the training that takes place in theological colleges and the skills and knowledge needed at the "grassroots ".

The third theme involved sustaining mission and vision. This matter was expressed in two forms. In one, it concerned institutional sustainability. So, for example, one participant asked, "Can we keep the doors open and the lights on if the government stops external money from entering the country?" In the second form, it concerned missional sustainability. "How can we remain true to our vision over the long haul?" I will comment on each of these themes in this order.

Theme One: Missional Integrity

The institutions studied are relatively young. At this stage in the life cycle of such institutions and movements, questions about missional integrity and institutional existence are to be expected.

Each organization began with a vibrant vision and great optimism. In order to implement their vision, strategies and structures came into being to facilitate it. But, as ministries expanded and the contexts within which that vision took form multiplied, new questions about the mission and its implementation necessarily arose. Comments such as the following represent common concerns: "We never thought about the need to gain credibility with the communities in which we labor. We never thought about all the questions we might be asked by Hindus. We never thought about how government policy might change and impact our work. We never thought about all it would take to get this done. After all, we were just going to train people to plant churches and then do it. What can be complicated about that?" In other words, over time circumstances forced ministries and institutions to return to and to probe their initial mission and vision in greater depth.

The point is that reexamining a movement's or an institution's mission should not be perceived as a threat. Rather, such activity is a normal, healthy, and necessary component of its missional life. Not to revisit that vision from time to time will eventually sound a ministry's death knell. Maintaining mission and vision *requires* regular revitalization that comes about through a prayerful reexamination of first principles and the manner in which they are being lived out.

Based on the self-examination prompted by the case studies and interrogation of those cases at the Consultation can only be considered "revitalization in progress". I cannot say it strongly enough. We witnessed revitalization in action through the process of raising and exploring questions of missional integrity. Although this activity occurred most visibly with the CEA study, we witnessed the same process ongoing with other studies as well.

Perhaps our participants from Nepal, being the youngest movement among all considered, have not yet reached the stage of necessary return to their mission and purpose. But the growing needs of followers of Christ in their country will bring them to this stage of life soon. When the time arrives, it should be welcomed and embraced.

In all of this, I commend the case participants for their humility. Undergoing such close examination and detailed probing is not easy. But the fruit that comes from Consultation would not be possible if not for a willingness to seek the Lord and to be faithfulness to His purposes.

Theme Two: Theological Training and the Grassroots

As with the paper as a whole, let me preface my treatment of this second them with one observation and comment before moving into more extended matters. I find it intriguing, in fact somewhat troubling, that I hear next to nothing about giftedness in the context of training for ministry. I hear it on good authority, namely the Apostle Paul, that God gives graces, gifts, and empowerment for various kinds of ministry (Ephesians 4:11-12). But I do not hear discussions about how such giftedness becomes identified, then nurtured and developed in students. I wonder why this subject is not more front and center, the starting point for discussion of training rather than an add on if it comes up at all.

Let's return to our questions regarding the connection between theological training and the needs of the grassroots. Let me put forward two theories about maintaining vitality in both spheres. I will integrate comments I heard during the consultation itself into my theoretical discussion.

Maintaining Appropriate Training Levels.

My first theory is that vitality in theological training is maintained when the level of education is appropriate for the level of the ministry in which the student is engaged. For example, in Case Study 4 (Chapter 6) with the Nepal group, someone mentioned five levels of leaders or leadership for which appropriate training was required.

1. Grassroots

2. Tentmakers

3. Overseers

4. State level

5. National level

These levels were not fully defined. But they point to different ministry settings that require different types of training, giftedness, and skill sets. Does training in a given theological college assume one or even two types of ministry skills/

knowledge only? A careful, honest process of assessment will be required in order to answer this question.

In a discussion in the CEA group, participants talked about training at satellite locations being a reproduction of what takes place at the NTC main campus. But the needs of a typical NTC student may not be the same as a student pastor in a satellite location. So if training is designed that assumes questions and issues that are not likely to be asked in the student's ministry and with knowledge that cannot be put to use in his or her setting, one risks pulling the life out of the ministry by the nature of theological training! We must think, therefore, about the spectrum of training appropriate to our student's ministries. Furthermore, we need flexibility to address the varied needs of the church as well as flexibility to address new needs as they arise.

This scenario is further complicated by the fact that the higher the degree offered, the higher the prestige associated with that degree. But more advanced degrees may train people for levels of ministry for which they are not a part.

This discussion of appropriate training raises additional questions. Does the structure and content of theological education arise from the top-down only, whether through accreditation requirements or the dictates of institutional leadership, or does it also respond to the needs of the ministry settings of graduates? Note that I presume neither a top-down nor bottom-up source for the structure and context of training. Rather, I contend input from both levels is necessary for appropriate theological education. Training derived from one source only risks courting a dangerous imbalance that will produce inappropriate training.

Addressing Appropriate Issues. Second, and related to the first, training must address appropriate issues. This was marvelously illustrated by the levels of what I call "experienced Christology" identified by the Filadelphia ministry among their members. These levels express a progression in understandings of Jesus held among those as they initially follow Christ (at the top of the list) and move toward additional conception reached over time as believers mature:

Jesus as healer

Jesus as exorcist

Jesus as protector

Jesus as provider

Jesus as savior

Jesus as Lord

Jesus as supreme God

Another way to depict this progression in understandings of Jesus moves through the following avenues, once again moving in order starting from the top:

Experience

Relationship

Knowledge

Reasoning

But, theological education typically operates in a movement in the opposite direction. Centered in a physical classroom and consisting of oral lectures, training emphasizes knowledge and reasoning, then assumes the student can translate this knowledge and reasoning into experience "at the grassroots". But Filadelphia's research on the their ministry settings shows that growth takes place through a process quite different than the one that structures theological education.

It was observed that Indian Christian Theology has traditionally been highly Brahman. I would say the same is true of the theology done in the West. But is that how people experience and come to understand Jesus? Do these insights tell us that we need to think in different terms about how we train people for ministry?

Obviously, I am arguing here for variants of contextual theology. Can we think of theological education, in general terms, as the process where biblical truth, practices, and character formation engage the questions, obstacles, and opportunities generated by the realities of life at the grassroots? In this case, how we practice theological education will always involve a conversation between, on the one hand, our knowledge and practices within the purposes of God honed over time, and the contextual questions and needs within which ministry takes place on the other. Theological knowledge at its best is knowledge that can be lived in dependence on the living God within the mission of the living God.

Theme Three: Sustaining Mission and Vision

Without question, one central dynamic for sustaining mission and vision is biblical leadership. I once heard it said (the source long since forgotten) that leaders need the wisdom of Solomon, the heart of a child, and the hide of a rhinoceros. No easy calling or task. Nor is it one that ready succumbs to succinct description. But here, in short, is a mere listing of worthy leadership traits that I overheard during the course of the Consultation.

Leaders of character. I heard over and over again about the character of founders. We witnessed the character of Uncle George, both his servant's heart and his gift of encouragement. But apart from character, leadership risks becoming self-serving— personal kingdom building rather than Kingdom of God building.

Leaders know their need of God. Perhaps nothing else expresses a qualification for leadership as does a life of prayer. Leaders who know their need of God, that understand ministry entrusted to his or her leadership comes from God, will be committed to prayer.

Leaders push those entrusted to their care to the edge of their comfort zones. If a leader's vitality is rooted in knowledge of his or her need of God, so is the vitality of a ministry or institution. Leaders will cast vision, then challenge people to live into that vision by God's enabling. Growth rarely take place within a comfort zone.

Leaders are other focused. Rooted in a life of prayer, leaders are less concerned with their own place or status than that of those entrusted to their leadership.

Leaders who continually narrate our place within the mission of God. Often called "casting vision," leaders continually focus on the big picture of God's calling for a ministry or institution rather than getting distracted by secondary matters. A prime task of leadership involves keeping all involved engaged in core business.

Leaders who will regularly review and revitalize the institution's or ministry's mission. Once again, leaders maintain focus on first things. Is the organization or movement really on target? Regular institutional self-examination is not seen as a threat but as an opportunity.

Final Remarks and a Look to the Future

By the end of the Consultation, several persistent conclusions about Christian revitalization seemed apparent. First, the need for Christian revitalization is not a sign of sin or mistakes or weakness. It can be, but we should not assume that is always the case. In fact, revitalization is a normal part of life with God for any ministry or institution (or individual for that matter). Intentional revisiting of a ministry's mission and vision for the purpose of furthering faithfulness to that mission and vision will often provide the spark that keeps the fires of God burning.

Second, we heard a remarkable, consistent theme of prayer and fasting. This was expressed marvelously in one of the sessions with the Nepal group, where one of the writers remarked that the first thing people are taught after conversion is prayer. This emphasis on prayer matches what we heard consistently in the case studies on revitalization in East Africa at a similar Consultation in Nairobi, Kenya, in 2013.

Third, and related to the second, we heard a remarkable, consistent theme of the miraculous power of God expressed in healing and deliverance. This points to a consistent openness to and dependence upon the Spirit of God. Once again this is consistent with what we heard in East Africa.

In addition, several facts point the direction toward Christian revitalizing work in the future. One participant reported that 65% of the population of India is under the age of 25. I imagine Nepal is no different. This tells me that to remain vital and relevant, to remain true to your mission and vision, you must pay serious attention to children and youth. Nurturing the gifts and developing the skills needed to reach and disciple such people must occupy a pivotal place in theological education and from there make its way into the churches.

Furthermore, while current estimates hold that 70% of India lives in rural regions, that will not be the case 20 years from now. Like most of the world, India and Nepal are rapidly urbanizing. In 20 years, the students presently in your churches and training centers will be in the prime of their ministries. By no means am I advocating closing down work in rural regions. But India and Nepal will become more urban and it will happen quickly. The culture of the future will be shaped by values and outlooks produced in those cities. And they will make their way to the countryside by means of the ubiquitous smart phones and other electronic media. Be ready. Begin thinking now about how best to prepare for a largely (though not exclusively) urban future.

I am deeply encouraged by what I witnessed over the course of the Consultation. The humility, commitment to prayer and fasting, persistence within difficult circumstances, but perhaps most of all, willingness to acknowledge weaknesses and mistakes, and then move on, provides the proper posture for God to renew your life.

I close with a story. A young man, hired by a bank in his early twenties, made his way rapidly up the corporate ladder of the institution. By the time he was in his mid-thirties, he displayed such leadership and managerial promise that he was asked to join the Board of the bank. When he was in his early forties, the aged and wizened President of the bank retired after long years in that office. Lo and behold, the young man was selected to become the new bank President. A bit intimidated by the task of replacing such a revered leader, he went to see the retiring President. After a brief conversation, he finally asked the elderly man, "What do I need to do to become a good President of the bank?" The President immediately replied, "Don't make mistakes." A bit taken aback, the young man paused, then asked, "How do I not make mistakes?" Once again the President's response was quick, "You need experience!" Feeling on the spot, given his relative youth, the young man persisted, "How do I get experience?" This time the President paused, then looked the young man squarely in the eyes and said slowly, "You make mistakes."

May your humility and firm trust in God keep you bold in living into your mission, never walking in fear of making mistakes. God will meet you in your faithful obedience.

www.ingramcontent.com/pod-product-compliance
Lightning Source LLC
Chambersburg PA
CBHW071451040426
42444CB00008B/1298